From Iror Coalbrc

Landed Gentry in Little Ness:

The Darby Family

Jessie E. Hanson

Published by

Peele Publishing

First published 2017

by Peele Publishing

Copyright © Jessie E. Hanson

All rights reserved

No part of this publication may be reproduced, stored in a retrieval system or transmitted in any form or by any means, electronic, mechanical, photocopying, recording or otherwise, without the prior written permission of the publisher and the copyright holder.

A catalogue record of this book is available from the British Library

Printed and bound by LIS Print Unit, University of Chester, Parkgate Road, Chester CH1 4BJ

ISBN 978-0-9934797-1-7

On a personal note

This book has been many years in the making and is partly the result of a number of talks given about the Darby family: their connection with Coalbrookdale, Little Ness and more particularly Adcote. It soon became obvious that although many people had heard of Abraham Darby, few realised there were in fact four Abraham's and they were just some of the individuals in a very talented family. Fewer people still, realised the connection between the Iron Bridge and Adcote, the grade 1 listed building in Little Ness designed by Norman Shaw. It is in an attempt to put both Adcote and Little Ness 'on the map', that this book came to fruition.

On a personal note, I have a much closer link with the Darby's for I grew up in Milford, only a short distance from Adcote and Little Ness. Frederica Darby knew all the local families, my mother included. My aunt, Alice Booth, actually worked for Frederica at Little Ness House before her marriage to the coachman. These are my own personal links with the local area.

There are a number of friends I wish to thank for their support and encouragement in writing about the Darby family, originally of Coalbrookdale, lately of Adcote.

Firstly, Dr Sharon Varey, who gave me so much support and encouragement throughout this project. Her advice and insight into the subject has been invaluable. Never one discouraging word, the perfect advisor and friend.

Ruth Campbell, who typed the original script, never once complaining on a re-write, another really good friend.

Barry Trinder, who introduced me to the work of the three Darby ladies and the writer of the first diary, Hannah Rose, neé Thomas.

Ruth Cook, who lent me her account of finding Maurice Darby's uniforms, left in the stables of Little Ness House.

Henry Quinn, who sent me information on Shropshire Banks.

Christine Cluely, who sent me a great deal of information on the paintings found in Little Ness Church.

Christine Abrams, with whom I had many interesting chats about the Darbys of Adcote.

Finally I should like to thank the many local people who had connections with Little Ness and the Darby Family, who shared their memories with me.

Jessie E. Hanson

Introduction

The Darby family of Coalbrookdale played a significant part in the Industrial Revolution in Britain. The story of their discoveries and the building of the World's first iron bridge is well known. However, there is a different, more intimate, side to this story which enhances our overall understanding of this prominent family.

Lady Labouchere, born Rachel Darby, and a direct descendant of Abraham Darby, discovered three journals or diaries in the family archives, written by female members of the family. She also discovered an earlier diary written by the daughter of an employee. Impressed by the information these journals contained, she decided to publish the diaries written by the Darby women. This proved a tremendous task and sadly, Lady Labouchere died before the third diary was complete. Emyr Thomas, who had been working closely with her, completed the last volume. Before her death, Lady Labouchere was President of the Ironbridge Gorge Museum Trust from 1973 until 1987 and willed Rosehill House and its contents, along with all the family papers and heirlooms she inherited from Muriel Cope Darby to the Trust as a permanent reminder of the Darby family.

The four diaries reveal the private lives of the Darby family and their contemporaries during the eighteenth and nineteenth centuries. They reveal the Darby family's devotion to their Quaker faith, their everyday living, along with the dreadful epidemics and disasters the family faced.

The earliest diary, written by Hannah Rose Thomas, has not been published. Hannah was the daughter of John Thomas who worked very closely with Abraham I, the founding father of the Darbys of Coalbrookdale. The other early diarists were Abiah and Deborah Darby. Staunch Quakers throughout their lives, religion would sometimes take priority and precedence over family life and serious illness. The women were well educated and in their

1

Quaker religion were regarded as equal to men. If they reached the approved standard they could become Ministers; something achieved by both Abiah and Deborah. In contrast to the other writers, the fourth diarist, Adelaide Darby, reveals how the family turned towards the Church of England in the nineteenth century and records family events at this time.

From the perspectives of these four women the personal family lives of the Darby family from their home in the Black Country to Coalbrookdale - scene of the greatest family triumphs and tragedies - to Little Ness - where they became country landowners - is revealed.

Beginnings

Abraham's father, John Darby, lived at Lodge Farm, Wren's Nest near Dudley in the Black Country. He was a small holder but he also had a furnace in his yard, so that during slack periods in the farming year, he could make small metal objects, such as nails and locks. Traders came and bought the metal objects which they then sold on at markets and fairs.

John married Ann Baylis and on 14 April 1678, a son, Abraham was born. Ester followed in 1680 but sadly John's wife Ann died shortly afterwards. John was left with two small children, a business and a small holding. In 1686 he married Joan Luccock of Halesowen. There were however, no children from this marriage.

Abraham Darby (1678 – 1717)

From a young age Abraham learnt the skills of metal working from his father so John looked for an Iron Master of the Quaker faith to apprentice him. He chose Jonathon Freeth, who was greatly respected for his standard of workmanship and his high regard within the Society of Friends. Freeth was a malt mill maker. Abraham duly worked for him, enhancing his skills, and completed his apprenticeship on 18 September 1699.

2

Now a qualified Iron Master, Abraham decided to move to Bristol where there was a large Quaker Community. There were many flourishing businesses and he joined the Bristol Brass and Iron Company at Baptist Mill which had been formed in 1702. In the early eighteenth century, the Netherlands had many thriving Ironworks and so Abraham was sent to Holland in 1704 to recruit additional workers. The company hoped that Dutch expertise would further develop the company's ironworking techniques. At this time the Brass and Wire Company were trying to cast hollow, round bottomed pots. With no breakthrough forthcoming, Abraham became disillusioned with the Dutch workers and decided to send them back to Holland as the company could not afford to pay wages without a return.

Having completed his apprenticeship, John Thomas, a young Welshman from Dolobran in mid Wales, had arrived in Bristol looking for work at the foundry. He had been orphaned and one of the local Quaker Lloyd family suggested Abraham Darby might give him work. Abraham realised the young man had great potential and employed him. John Thomas joined Abraham in his quest to cast an iron pot in sand. Here began a life-long friendship. They worked together in great secrecy, to the extent of blocking the keyhole so that nothing of their experiments could be given away! They succeeded in casting the pot and John Thomas signed an agreement promising not to divulge the secret for three years. The patent, No. 380, was signed on 18 April 1707. John was to be paid £7 per annum for the first 2 years and £8 in his last year. He was to be provided with sufficient good meat, drink, washing and lodging. After the signing of the patent and the breakthrough, Abraham could foresee an entirely new approach to casting metal and a flourishing future. The patent gave him time to develop the new technique. Surprisingly, the other Bristol partners did not seem to understand the significance of this breakthrough. This allowed Abraham to break the partnership and strike out on his own, confident that he could mass produce the pots and develop his ideas still further. He decided to form an independent company and began to look for new premises. All he needed was a suitable site for development.

Round bottomed iron pot

The River Severn was a great highway for trading and the exchange of news. Word came that there was a disused furnace in Coalbrookdale in Shropshire, belonging to the Basil Brookes estate. It was leased to Shadrock Fox who was no longer able to use it for the furnace had exploded when water from the flooded River Severn had seeped in. On inspection, Abraham realised that it was an ideal site with easy access to the river and a number of coal mines in the area with limestone quarries at nearby Benthall and Wenlock. The lease was transferred to Abraham.

In the past there had been plenty of woodland for charcoal but many local woods were seriously depleted. Abraham believed he could use coke as he had done when he was a malt miller and he soon discovered that the quality of the coal from these surface mines was suitable for coking. Fortunately, a local labour force was readily available for there were no other large places of work for the local people. In addition, a number of his own workforce had chosen to move with their families to Coalbrookdale for Abraham was a respected, kind employer. The Bristol workforce were Quakers and brought their ideas of worship with them.

Abraham's business flourished so he encouraged his father and step-mother to join him in Coalbrookdale. Although Joan was blind she was able to run the house and spin. Meanwhile, Abraham's sister, Ester, had married a farmer, Anthony Parker, described as a sober and honest man. The Coalbrookdale Ironworks had farm land attached, so Ester and Anthony came to live on one of the farms. This particular farm had a cart track running through it and the track continued through a neighbour's land. Regarded locally as a 'right of way,' Abraham used the track to transport his goods, infuriating the neighbouring farmer. The farmer was so angered that he shouted that he'd never speak again if Quaker horses and carts continued to use the track. Abraham rose to the challenge, sending more carts down the track. The farmer was so impassioned that he was lost for words. The likelihood is that he had a stroke because, true to his word, he never spoke again!

Although there was a Quaker Meeting House in Broseley by 1692, only a few of the local inhabitants were Quakers. The above episode reveals that Quakers were regarded by some local people as outsiders and not welcome. By 1716, Madeley parish had eight Quaker families, all working for Abraham.

Abraham married Mary Sargeant in 1699 in Dudley, Worcestershire. Her father was Joshua Sargeant, a Quaker linen bleacher. Abraham and Mary had five sons and six daughters. A terrible accident occurred one day when Mary visited the Ironworks. Somehow she slipped into a vat of hot metal.

Workmen ran to the vat and miraculously got her out and laid her on the ground, convinced she was dead. To everyone's astonishment Mary recovered. Possibly her thick clothing had saved her. As she recovered, she recounted an 'out of world' experience. She related that she had been met by two angels, who escorted her to a very fine place, finer than anything in this world, that she had so swiftly left. She was preparing to stay in that glorious world but was told she would be returning to the everyday one. The experience so influenced her earthly life that she became very religious. Although there is no mention of severe scaring or suffering from burns, Mary suffered from asthma for the rest of her life and as a result often sat up all night to relieve it.

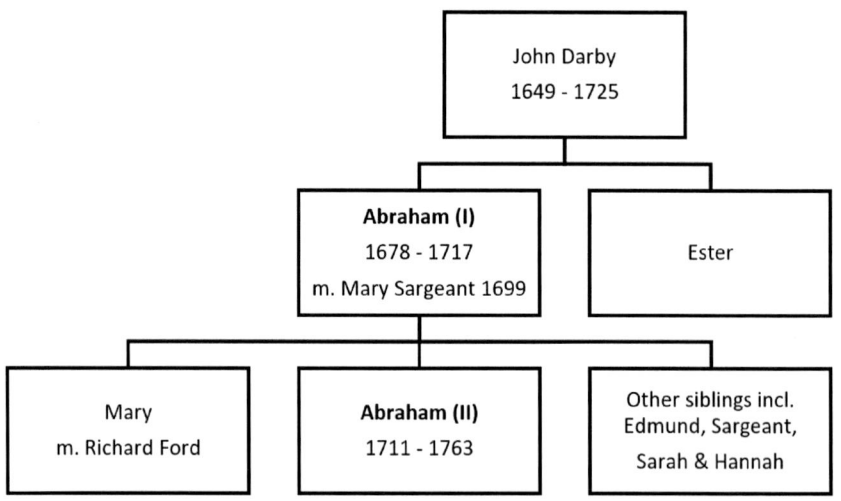

Family tree showing Abraham I and II

At Coalbrookdale, Mary and Abraham lived in a timber framed house known as White End. As the family grew, they needed a larger house. They rented half of a large mansion known as Madeley Court which was owned by Basil Brookes. Madeley Court was the ideal house for bringing up children. It was spacious inside and had plenty of land outside, including a medieval fishpond which often froze in winter enabling the children to slide on the ice. The house had originally been the summer residence of the priors of Wenlock Abbey. Following the Dissolution, Thomas Brookes, a Catholic, bought it and added extra rooms. Many of the rooms were oak panelled and had priest holes. One was discovered behind the oak panelling in the chapel.

Madeley Court

As the business prospered, Abraham found Madeley Court too far from the Ironworks, so he decided to build a new house near the furnace as was the custom of Iron Masters. The site chosen was on the west bank of the valley near the furnace pool. The house 'was built slowly of good old oak and bricks.'

The Ironworks continued to expand and further furnaces were built. John Thomas was in charge of one of the moulding shops at the upper furnace. In 1714, he returned to Bristol to marry Grace Zean and when they returned to Coalbrookdale they moved into White End. They had four children, John, George and Samuel and the diarist, Hannah. Without her diary, much of this early family background, and that of the Darby family, would be unknown.

Abraham remained true to his Quaker faith. He regularly met William Osborne and together they attended Quaker meetings. Abraham bought a piece of land in Broseley which was turned into a Quaker burial ground. Unfortunately the site caused problems, especially in bad weather, as it was situated up a steep hill. Sometimes it proved too steep for the coffin bearers and older members of the funeral procession to reach the burial ground.

During the last eighteen months of his life, Abraham was a sick man. It is possible he had lung cancer. Although unwell, he ran the Coalbrookdale Ironworks and continued to work for the Society of Friends. Abraham held Quaker Services in his unfinished house, then known as the 'New House' but later renamed Dale House. A good description of Abraham's last days can be found in Hannah Rose's diary:

> The meeting he was at was in the New House which he had built at Coalbrookdale. It was not quite finished, so not inhabited. The meeting was held in a room now called the best parlour and he was greatly favoured in prayer. My father and mother said they had never heard as fine and he was too ill to sit the meeting out.

Mary Darby later wrote about the last distressing hours of Abraham's life. Talking about his close friend, John Thomas, she wrote:

> He stood at my dying husband's side and heard his mind and as much as I cared for him when poor and of low estate, has in these later troubles been to me as a son.

It was unusual for a master and his family to form such a close friendship with an employee.

Abraham died on the 5 May 1717 and was buried two days later. The small six year old Abraham II led the funeral procession to the Quaker graveyard. The procession crossed the River Severn by boat and then made its way up the steep hill to the burial ground in Broseley where he was laid to rest. Years later, Abiah wrote: 'My husband's father died early in life, a religious good man and an eminent minister amongst the people called Quakers.'

Trouble brewing

Both Thomas Baylis and Richard Ford joined the Coalbrookdale Company in 1714. No one realised at the time that these appointments would play such a significant part in the future of the Company.

Although initially recruited as a clerk, Abraham realised Richard Ford had great potential and gradually gave him more and more responsibility in the running of the company. He was trained by Abraham to adopt an enterprising attitude to running the Ironworks. He came from Stourbridge where his father, Edmund, was a Tallow Chandler. By the time Abraham died in 1717, Richard was an important figure in the company.

Abraham died intestate, so Mary took out Letters of Administration. Thomas Goldney was owed £1600 for which Abraham had mortgaged half the Ironworks. Mary was unable to repay Thomas Goldney so the value of the Ironworks was divided into sixteen shares each worth £200. Eight were assigned to Thomas Goldney and two were sold to Richard Ford. Unfortunately trouble was brewing, for Thomas Baylis, Mary's brother-in-law, announced that he was owed an outstanding debt of £1200. He therefore claimed Mary Darby's six shares in the Coalbrookdale works leaving Mary and her children with no shares in the Ironworks. Baylis then obtained Letters of Administration for himself, claiming that he was the survivor of a joint tenancy. Baylis's cruelty towards Mary and her family knew no bounds: he refused to allow her to move into New House, instead forcing her to move back into the old house where she had begun her married life. Baylis then moved into New House.

As a result of this, Mary's brother, Joshua Sargeant, called Thomas Goldney and other friends of Abraham to a meeting where they discussed how to resolve Mary Darby's plight. Fortunately, for the future of the company, Baylis got himself into financial difficulties. This allowed Thomas Goldney and his son to purchase his shares. Nevertheless, the situation had become too much for Mary and she left Coalbrookdale for Bewdley to stay with family and friends. Sadly she died on 1 April 1718, less than a year after Abraham. She was buried in Bewdley, far away from Abraham who had been buried in Broseley.

At the time of Mary's death, Thomas Goldney held most of the shares in the company. Thomas, his son, held one share and Richard Ford held two. Richard Ford and Thomas Goldney II succeeded in moving Baylis out of New House. They eventually proved that Baylis had forged Abraham's signature on a number of documents. He did not move quietly, printing a long account of his grievances! Baylis then crossed to North America and set up an Ironworks which he named Coalbrookdale. The enterprise failed.

Hannah Rose says of Baylis:

> He proved to be a very bad man, borrowed money
> in Abraham Darby's name, and my father was
> cheated and other workmen by him.

On 1 August 1718, Richard Ford married Abraham's daughter Mary. They became the official guardians of Mary and Abraham's children and brought the orphaned family back to Dale House (formerly New House) in Coalbrookdale, having forced Baylis and his family to leave. After settling into their family home, Mary and Richard began looking for a suitable Quaker school to send their siblings. They thought the school run by Gilbert Thompson and his son in Penketh, Lancashire most suitable for 'the curriculum and discipline under both father and son seems very enlightened.' The children, while still young, would be together although they would be away from their adult family for long periods, for they only returned home during the summer holidays. Abraham, Edmund, Sergeant and Sarah would have left Coalbrookdale dressed in the simple Quaker style. Clothing was home-made and of a plain style and material.

Edmund and Abraham's school fees were £30 per year. One school account records wigs purchased for the boys, costing £1 6s 0d. It was at school that Abraham met his life-long friend, Samuel Fothergill, brother of the famous Doctor John Fothergill. Luckily one of Abraham's Maths exercise books survives. Bound in vellum, the problems encompass weights and measures, circumference, rates of exchange between Great Britain and the continent. School work was tailored to suit the industrial workplace.

Sadly Abraham's other siblings died young: Sergeant in 1725, Sarah in 1726 and Hannah the following year.

Abraham II

Young Abraham left school at 17 and joined Richard Ford at the Coalbrookdale foundry. Abraham learned about the general administration of the works, the pattern of trade and banking practice. Abraham was a willing worker and gradually Richard Ford let him take over. Thomas Goldney senior, the principal Coalbrookdale shareholder, died in 1731. His son, Thomas Goldney II, indicated that the business would continue as his father had directed. Richard and Abraham worked well together and in 1732 he became Richard's assistant. The Trustees gave Abraham a gold watch to reflect his position at the Ironworks. Abraham was sent to Trade Fairs to broaden his experience and in 1733 he represented the company in Chester. In order to expand his knowledge and increase his Quaker connections still further, Abraham was sent to large markets throughout Great Britain and he was often invited to stay with Quaker families.

It was at this time that Abraham became a partner. His younger brother, Edmund, became an apprentice living with Richard Ford. A bill of 1734 states that the latter received £52 10s 0d for his board and instruction. In 1734, at the age of 23, Abraham's salary increased to £50 per year, plus the interest from the family shares. He was now able to contemplate marriage. The Darby family often visited Shifnal to attend Quaker meetings and it was here he met Margaret Smith and they married. One of the wedding guests described Abraham as: 'small and slight of stature, very active and strong. His eyes are black and very bright and his complexion dark.'

Abraham and Margaret lived at Dale House while the Fords moved to nearby Rosehill. A daughter, Hannah, was born in 1735 and this was soon followed by two sons, Abraham (1736) and Edmund (1738). Both boys died in 1740 and this was followed by the death of their mother Margaret later that same year. Abraham's sister Mary (Ford) came to his rescue to help bring up Hannah, just as she had looked after Abraham and his siblings after their mother's death. Hannah proved to be an affectionate child, lively, intelligent and naturally became the centre of Abraham's life.

Dale House

Rosehill

Abraham met his second wife, Abiah, in Kendal whilst visiting the home of Robert and Grace Chamber. Abiah belonged to the wealthy Maude family from Sunderland. They were mining engineers and owners of numerous coal mines and considerable property. The family claimed to be descended from Henry III and Eleanor of Castile.

Abiah was a devout Quaker who put her religion above everything. Before she met Abraham, she had fallen in love with John Sinclair, an impoverished Quaker Minister and wished to marry him. This upset her mother because he was of much lower social status than Abiah's family and so she was very reluctant to approve of their marriage. Nevertheless, they married and had a daughter who was baptised, Rachel. Sadly, John Sinclair contracted smallpox and died. Later, Rachel also died of smallpox. Abiah was devastated. Heartbroken, she turned inwardly to her Quaker religion for help.

Abiah was good looking, intelligent and had a pleasant personality. Abraham fell in love with her, and tried to persuade her to marry him. She did not accept, but neither did she reject outright his proposals of marriage. Abiah felt her religion must take precedence over everything. Abraham was persistent and followed her over England, meeting her at Quaker gatherings. Abiah's closest friends could see that Abraham would make a good husband and pointed out his suitability. He too had lost his previous partner in an epidemic and was left with a daughter. Her friends also felt that he would understand and encourage Abiah's religious beliefs. Above all, they considered that Abraham had a suitable temperament and an excellent position in society. Eventually she conceded and agreed with her friends that he would make an ideal husband.

Abiah accepted Abraham's proposal and they were married at Preston Patrick Meeting House on 9 March 1745. The wedding was simple with a number of friends and family from the Coalbrookdale area attending.

Twenty two horses were ridden back to Coalbrookdale after the wedding. The newly-weds returned to live in Dale House. Abiah was fully accepted into the Darby family and touchingly Abraham's daughter Hannah called her 'Mother.'

Abiah, as a new wife, had to cope with an influx of family, friends and business people. It required considerable organisational ability to accommodate and entertain the visitors but it was vitally important to the company. Abraham and Abiah's first child, Rachel, was born in December 1746 after a difficult pregnancy for Abiah suffered from 'military fever,' a condition whereby she lost the use of her limbs. Fortunately this was a temporary loss, but very sadly baby Rachel died at fifteen weeks. Mary, their second child, was born in 1748. Luckily this was a much easier birth. On 24 April 1751 a son, Abraham, followed. He was the last of her children to be born in Dale House as Abiah and Abraham decided to build a new house, higher up the valley on the bridleway to Little Wenlock.

The house was called 'Sunniside', named after Abiah's family home in Bishop's Wear, Sunderland, where she had spent a happy childhood. Sunniside was built using locally made bricks and was faced with stone. It was planned as a mini estate with landscaped grounds, malt houses, breweries, stables, barns and workmen's cottages.

Now happily married and settled, Abraham's life revolved around the Ironworks. In 1756 Abraham was able to buy out his partners, making him free to develop the works as he wished. He experimented using coke to smelt iron. Convinced that he could use this method, he worked non-stop day and night perfecting his new ideas. On one occasion he stayed up for six days and nights and as a result he fell to the ground unconscious. Luckily, Abraham soon recovered and continued experimenting. At last he succeeded in smelting iron ore into pig iron – another first for the Darby family.

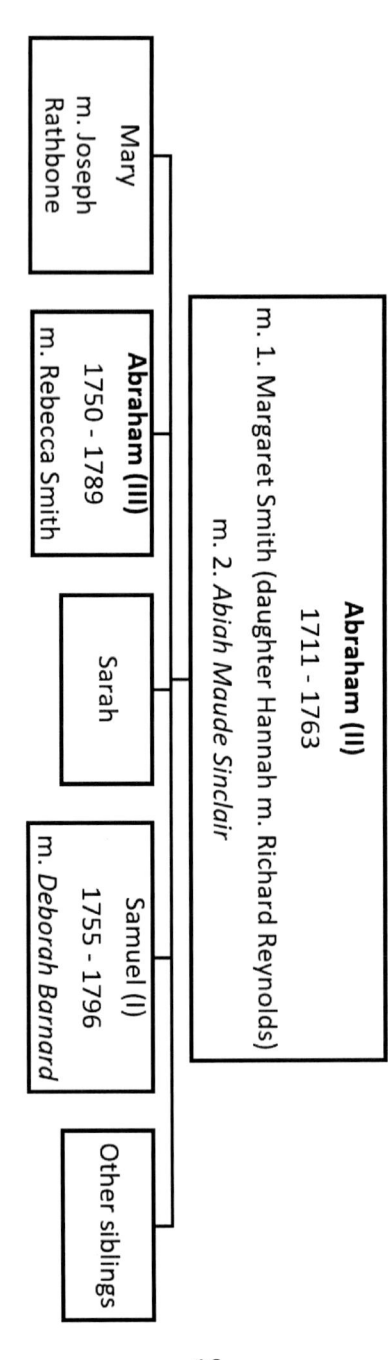

Family tree showing Abraham II and III
(diarists are shown in italics)

Abraham II sent his new product to selective buyers to seek their reaction. The product was well received and he received new orders. In order for the company to expand further, Abraham needed a new furnace. He built new furnaces at Horsehay but the water supply proved unreliable. To ensure a constant supply of water, he installed a Newcomb engine which enabled the water to be recycled. In January 1757 the first load of pig iron was brought by rail from the Horsehay works to Coalbrookdale. The wagons were a new style for the area, cauldron shaped, very like the tubs used by the Maude family on their Newcastle coalfields. Many people came to see the new forge and railway.

Abraham showed great enterprising spirit, for he founded iron foundries in London, Bristol and Liverpool, with agencies in Newcastle upon Tyne and Truro. These were areas which needed machinery to pump water from the tin and coal mines. He continued to experiment using different combinations of coal to make the perfect coke. South Shropshire coke proved to be ideal for casting iron due to its low sulphur content.

Unfortunately 1757 was a year of family tragedies. In February, Abiah wrote that her cousin Darby Ford fell into New Pool and was drowned. The body was recovered the next day causing the family much distress. On 2 March he was buried in the Quaker Graveyard at Broseley. At the beginning of June, Abraham's brother Edmund fell from his horse when returning from Abingdon Fair. He fractured his skull and subsequently died from his injuries.

Sadness was mingled with joy this year with the marriage of Abraham's daughter, Hannah to Richard Reynolds in May. Richard was born into a Quaker family in Bristol in 1735. At the age of 14 he was apprenticed to William Fry, a grocer. Completing his apprenticeship in 1757, he was then made a freeman of Bristol like his father. He was employed by Thomas Goldney, the rich and influential Bristol Quaker, whose family were close friends with the Darbys. Richard had a good brain, long brown hair, good looks and a charming personality. Hannah and Richard were immediately attracted to one another and were married on the 20 May at the Shrewsbury Meeting House. Following the ceremony they returned to Coalbrookdale where a party was held at Sunniside. The newlyweds went to live in a house at Ketley Bank, near the Horsehay works, where Richard was Manager. Hannah and Richard went on to have two children: William and Hannah Mary. Sadly, William contracted smallpox and died.

During the summer of 1757 there was great distress locally. This was caused by the high price of bread and other food shortages. Hannah Darby wrote in a letter to her aunt:

> The colliers at Broseley, Madeley Wood and at the Darby coalmines were very restive. The men were blowing horns, this was a signal to march. They decided to target the markets selling corn. They descended on Wenlock market and confronted the farmers. The conditions they set out was either to sell their corn at five shillings per bushel or have it taken from them. Two hours were given for the farmers to decide. When some farmers refused, the colliers took the wheat from them. Next morning they forced old Judge Jordan to ride with them to Shifnal market. In town they plundered houses and barns taking everything they could.

Hannah noted that some of the Dale miners were among the rioters. The following day the rioters met at Broseley and gave loud huzzas to drown out a proclamation read to them. The situation did not improve and some men turned up at the Dale Ironworks threatening to destroy the works if they were not given food and drink. They also threatened to harm the workers if they did not agree to march with them to Wellington the following day.

Abraham gave one of his clerks 20 guineas to give to the ring leaders. Other men were sent to the lower gate to distribute money, ale and bread. This action probably saved the Ironworks and Darby houses from attack. The rioters left for Wellington market, breaking into houses on their way and taking silver, pewter and any other goods of value. Later it was learned that Sunniside was listed to be raided that day. Four Darby workmen were arrested at Wellington market. The punishment for rioting was either transportation or hanging. Abraham wrote to Lord Gower pleading their cause, pointing out that they had been exemplary workmen for him, but what happened to the men is not known.

During his life Abraham II invested well. His company at Coalbrookdale now had its own tile and brick works, along with coal and ironstone mines in Dawley, Lawley and Little Wenlock and limestone quarries in Bridgnorth. In addition to his Shropshire premises, Abraham had numerous interests outside the county.

By 1763 Abraham realised he was terminally ill and on 17 February he sent for his lawyer to prepare his will. He set up a Trust for his family covering the shares he owned in the Coalbrookdale, Horsehay, Ketley, Lawley, Dawley and Benthall Ironworks and all his other works in Great Britain. However, Sunniside and the adjacent land was not covered. Abiah was to have £2000 at her disposal and Sunniside for life. This included possession of all the household goods and livestock which she was free to dispose of how she wished. Additionally, she was to have an annuity of £300 and to be given custody of the children. Each child was given an allowance and their education was to be paid for until the age of 21. Upon reaching 21, the children were to be given £2000 shares at 5%. His son Abraham was to have a half share in Hay Farm and land in Madeley. His son Samuel was to have the house and garden he had bought from Richard Ford when he became bankrupt. Abraham additionally left various sums of money to his friends.

In March, Abiah became very concerned with, 'my dear husband's illness.' William Maude, Abiah's nephew who was visiting at the time, wrote home that Abraham was growing weaker and was not fit to discuss business. Abraham's health declined further and he died. Abiah wrote:

> My dear husband departed this life and entered into rest, his peace was great. Love and innocence manifested in him and patience reigned. ... The loss to the community, to our Society and myself and family is very great.

> My dear husband's remains were entered in a piece of ground, which he in his illness, pointed out and directed us how we should direct his corpse to it.

This 'special' resting ground could be seen from the window of Sunniside and lay beyond the little deer park. Abiah comments that Abraham chose this spot, 'with the greatest calmness and composure'. Abraham was the first Quaker to be buried in this new burial ground.

Many friends attended the funeral and there were numerous testimonies to him but to Abiah he was 'in private life an affectionate husband and tender parent, a kind master and a steady friend.'

Abiah was now the matriarch of the family, overseeing the bringing up of the children, the welfare of the workforce, offering continual hospitality at Sunniside. Over time she became known as 'Mother Darby'.

The 'new' burial ground

Abraham III

Following Abraham's death, Goldney, Beasley and Brooks arrived at Sunniside to discuss the contents of Abraham's will and the day-to-day running of the Coalbrookdale Works. Abraham Darby III was only 11 years old, so there was no-one within the Darby family to take over the management of the Ironworks. This position was taken by Richard Reynolds who had originally come to Shropshire on behalf of Thomas Goldney II's interests in the company. Reynolds moved into Dale House at the end of

August. He was a considerate employer: 'his relation with the work people continued the policy of the Darbys, complete friendliness and care for their well-being.' This included continuing the Darby family's policy in providing houses for their employees. Under Reynolds management, the company and its numerous purchases flourished.

Sadly, Richard Reynold's beloved wife Hannah died, leaving him alone with two small children. After a while he decided to remarry, and, with Abiah's approval, approached Hannah's close friend, Rebecca Gulson, asking for her hand in marriage. She accepted and proved to be the ideal wife and step-mother. They were married in Coventry on 1 December 1763. Happily married once more, Reynolds was able to concentrate on the business of the Ironworks.

Once Abraham was 18 he was brought into the works under Reynold's care and ultimately was to count him, not only as his partner, but his dearest friend and adviser. Some years later Abraham's younger brother, Samuel, joined him. During their life time there was great expansion in the Darby enterprise. Their sister Mary, married Joseph Rathbone who managed the Coalbrookdale business in Liverpool. Abraham III had a great interest in merchant shipping and when he was of age owned a quarter share in the ship, 'Darby,' which traded from Liverpool to the Baltic possibly with Coalbrookdale goods, returning with a timber cargo.

In 1776, Abraham married Rebecca Smith. She was the niece of Rebecca Reynolds and had often stayed at Coalbrookdale. Her father Francis was a grocer and she had been well educated. Before their marriage, Abraham had given her a pair of sleeve buttons beautifully presented in an oval box lined with white satin. The buttons were gold with dark blue enamelled scrolling. This expensive gift was contrary to Quaker principles but she appreciated the beautiful jewellery.

The marriage took place at the Quaker Meeting House in Warnsworth in the county of York. All Rebecca's family were present and Abiah brought the immediate Darby family. There were also a large number of friends and other relations as well. Abraham and Rebecca returned to live in Dale House in Coalbrookdale which over-looked the original furnace. Three months later there was another Darby wedding as Abraham's brother Samuel married Deborah Barnard.

Samuel Darby I

Abraham's younger brother Samuel was the last of Abiah and Abraham II's children to be born at Sunniside. Born on 16 January 1755, Abiah was very protective towards her youngest child.

Small pox was a disease that was dreaded as it killed both young and old. By the 1750s innoculations were being performed by some more enlightened doctors. The idea of inoculation had been introduced by Lady Mary Worsley, wife of the British Ambassador to Turkey, upon her return to England in 1718. Initially, both medical and religious leaders were against the procedure but the idea gradually gained popularity. It was not a pleasant procedure for it was a long and painful process, but in most cases it worked. Samuel was taken by Abiah with other Darby cousins to stay with the Doctor at Buildwas. The inoculation was performed between 4 and 5 pm in the afternoon. A large needle was taken and three or four veins opened. The best smallpox matter, the size of a nutshell, was taken and placed on the open wound. Signs of a reaction followed about eight days later and this was followed by a mild attack of the disease. Upon recovery, the patient could go home; they would then be immune when the next epidemic broke out. All the Darby children were successfully inoculated in this way.

Like most Quakers, Abraham and Abiah felt that health, happiness and a good education were of the greatest importance in children's lives. It was decided to send Samuel to John Fells School in Worcester, where other family members had been educated. It was easily accessible by the River Severn, or by road. There were many Quaker families in Worcester which the boys would be introduced to, either at school or through Quaker friends.

Upon leaving school Samuel embarked upon an apprenticeship at the Coalbrookdale Ironworks in Liverpool. Joseph Rathbone, who had married Abraham and Samuel's sister, Mary, was in charge of the works. Liverpool was a very different environment from the other Darby Ironworks. Here many of the Quaker families ran companies with overseas connections. At first Samuel lived with his sister and brother-in-law. Mary, before her marriage, had been his mother's companion and confident.

Samuel completed his apprenticeship and it was decided he should move to the Darby's London Ironworks, to take charge. His sister, Sarah, an intelligent, strong and resilient character, decided to accompany Samuel and run his household. She became his great support through this early life of responsibility. In London he was assisted by Wilson Birbeck, a member of a wealthy Quaker family from Yorkshire, whose family had a woollen and general merchants business in Settle and a banking and insurance business in London. Birkbeck became Samuel's clerk and chief assistant. When he came of age in April 1776, the Executor's Trust Fund (set up for the children of Abraham II) expired and Samuel became responsible for his own shares in the company and his inheritance. This meant that Samuel became a full partner with his brother in the Coalbrookdale Company.

Whilst in Liverpool, Samuel met Deborah Barnard, a cousin of Wilson Birbeck. Samuel was attracted to Deborah, but he was considered too young for marriage. He was however considered a suitable candidate for the future. There is an interesting description of Samuel at this time. Mary Knowles, in a letter to her cousin, observed that if the marriage took place

> it was likely to prove a very happy one for ... the young man was wealthy and handsome, sensible and religious, dutiful to his parents, affectionate to his relations, kind and liberal to mankind in general.

Samuel had artistic and literary tastes and was an avid collector of books. Already he owned a small library and had designed his own bookplate 'Samuel Darby, London'. Amongst his collection of classical and religious books, he owned the 1669 publication of *No Cross, No Crown* written by William Penn. His character was such that he would have suited an academic life, rather than the unpredictable rigours of manufacturing and commerce.

Deborah was born on 25 August 1754 at Upperthorpe, to the north east of Sheffield. This was an industrial area, cutlery being the chief product. Her father, John Barnard, was a tanner who belonged to the Hartshead Quaker Meeting. Deborah's mother was Hannah Wilson from Kendal, whose family were engaged in the wool and leather trade. Her grandmother was a friend of Abiah Darby and had visited her at Coalbrookdale. Interestingly, her sister, Rachel, was married to Isaac Wilson who had made the journey to North America in 1768 as a Quaker Minister.

The wedding took place on 2 August 1776 in Sheffield. A large number of family and friends attended the marriage. The Coalbrookdale group, including Abiah, travelled back together to Sunniside. After resting, Deborah and Samuel rode on to London, to run the Company's Ironworks. Abiah's sister, who had recently been widowed, accompanied the family group back to Shropshire.

The following year, Deborah gave birth to a son, who was named Abraham. He was a delicate baby who was subject to fits. Abiah had great faith in the healing power of amber cakes. She made some and sent them to Deborah along with the recipe. Sadly, the cakes did not improve the child's condition and he died in the summer of 1778.

At this time the London Ironworks were in trouble and seemed likely to close. Business failure was considered a serious weakness by the Quaker community. Samuel, of course, was very upset about the failure of the business and his health began to fail. It may have been the intense pressure and responsibility he carried as a working Iron Master which contributed to his deep depression, or he might have suffered from bi-polarism. Whatever the exact cause, Samuel suffered from periods of ill-health and instability throughout his life; at times having to be taken from his family for his own protection. At this point in time, he had to attend a number of meetings which could not have been easy because it was decided to sell the Ironworks. On 29 November a letter arrived from London telling them of the foundry sale. Deborah commented that she was 'glad our outward concerns are lessening.'

There followed a hectic time at Sunniside as Samuel decided to leave London and live with his mother in Shropshire. His sister Sarah went to London to supervise the packing of the furniture, books and household goods. The decision was made to make two separate households, but to eat their main meal of the day together. To add to the household complications the Rathbones also moved to Sunniside while they waited for Dale House to be made ready for their occupation. Abiah must have been pushed to her limit providing accommodation for the families, their servants and, possibly other visitors. The following year, Samuel II was born at Sunniside. He developed fits like Abraham but fortunately he recovered from them and grew up strong and healthy.

All too soon, Deborah became unwell having begun another pregnancy. She was very close to her father, who realised the intense pressure his daughter was under. Understanding her family problems and her great love of nature, he had a cottage retreat built for her in a wood. The situation enabled her to put her worries to one side and totally relax. A couple, who lived in part of the house, took care of it for her. Deborah gave birth to a daughter on 4 August, but sadly she only lived for 12 hours.

However, in the spring of 1782 Edmund was born and Deborah made a fine recovery. She travelled to London in June to be with her husband Samuel who was poorly, but when she arrived, she was not allowed to see him. Deborah now had two small children and the additional worries of a very ill husband along with their business concerns. Although this was a lengthy breakdown, Samuel recovered and returned to join his brother Abraham in running the Coalbrookdale works.

Deborah's diary reveals that she found her husband's bouts of instability difficult to cope with and often left others to deal with them. Deborah considered her Quaker religion paramount in her life and it took precedence over everything, including her family. At times she would leave her husband and children, to follow the call of Ministry, because, like Abiah, she too became a Quaker Minister. She did a great deal of travelling throughout her life, visiting various parts of the British Isles and also the English colonies in North America on a number of occasions.

The children, Samuel and Edmund were sent to school in Burford. The school was run by Mr and Mrs Huntley. Burford was an important stop on the stage coach route for changing horses. Enterprisingly, Mrs Huntley took advantage of this to supplement the income from the school by making biscuits to sell to the stage coach travellers. Such were the humble beginnings of the Huntley and Palmer biscuit company!

The building of the bridge

The idea of bridging the River Severn in the area of Coalbrookdale had been discussed many times for the increasing industrialisation of the Severn Gorge necessitated the need for a bridge to span the river. There were ferries for foot and light goods, but they were not always reliable, as floods and droughts often affected the water level. The large number of barges that used the river meant that a bridge would need a single large span. Following a meeting in Broseley, a committee was set up to forward the proposal for the construction of a suitable bridge. Firstly an Act of Parliament was needed to obtain permission to bridge the river. Abiah's family, the Maudes, had a relative who was an MP. They were consulted for advice and guided the necessary Bill through Parliament. Once this had been achieved, tenders were sought through advertisements in the local Shrewsbury and Birmingham newspapers.

So, aged just 26, Abraham III embarked upon an entirely new project to build a single span bridge of iron. With his tender accepted, Abraham needed to find responsible and innovative individuals to design the bridge, cast the iron and design abutments which could withstand the force of the river in flood. None of these were easy tasks.

Whilst Abiah's sister was staying at Coalbrookdale, following Samuel's wedding, she wrote to her family mentioning the new bridge which would span the River Severn.

> The Bridge to be built at the bottom of the Dale is now fixed upon to be an iron one, which certainly when completed will be the greatest curiosity this Nation can boast of, I think. There is two years allowed for finishing it. I suppose it will be cast in the Dale for cousin Abraham will have the whole direction.

How accurately she predicted the impact the Iron Bridge would have all over the world.

The first person to be engaged was Thomas Farnolds Pritchard who was chosen as the architect to work closely with Abraham. Thomas was the son of Hannah and John Pritchard of Shrewsbury. He was baptised on 11 May 1723 at St Julian's Church, Shrewsbury. Little is known of his early life but it is thought he had been apprenticed to a stone mason. His father was a joiner, who taught him to work with wood. Around 1750 he began to practice as an architect and surveyor. In August 1751 he married Elinor Russel at St Julian's Church, Shrewsbury. He had a workshop and yard in Ox Lane, Shrewsbury – an area now known as St Mary's Street. In 1769 he moved to Eyton-on-Severn with his family. He worked on numerous projects in and around Shrewsbury, co-ordinating teams of highly skilled craftsmen. His business thrived and much of his work can still be seen in Shrewsbury today. Sadly, Thomas Farnolds Pritchard died one month before the bridge was completed.

Pritchard engaged a local carpenter named Gregory to make a wooden model of the proposed bridge. There had been much discussion on the length of the bridge's span. Firstly 130 feet was suggested, but eventually a span of 90 feet was agreed. Each individual section was initially made to scale, in mahogany, to the exact design. The model was then carefully assembled. Abraham and his team of ironworkers had to calculate if each section would be strong enough to carry the weight of the road and local traffic. Today the wooden model of the bridge can be seen at the Science Museum in London.

As the existing furnaces were needed for the Company's on-going day-to-day trade contracts, an additional furnace was needed to cast each piece of the bridge. In October 1776 Abraham bought the Madeley Wood furnace, to produce the iron and cast each piece for the bridge. The furnace worked day and night, lighting up the night sky, throwing out flames, smoke and steam, and earned the name 'Bedlam.'

Each section of the bridge had to be designed accurately so that the pieces slotted together easily yet could carry immense weight. When cast, each section was brought to the river bank and placed in the order they would be used. The first sections to be erected were the stone abutments on each side of the river, for these were needed to support the metal structure. Ropes were attached to the metal castings and these were hauled onto the scaffolding and then put into place. Abraham and his workforce had faith in each other and gradually the iron bridge was assembled.

The Iron Bridge

December 1779 saw the scaffolding removed and the world's first iron bridge was revealed. It was a beautiful structure spanning the river, high enough for trows to sail under and strong enough to allow all sizes of carts and horse drawn vehicles to cross. There was only one small doubt, would it withstand a surge of water when the River Severn flooded?

The bridge was formerly opened on New Year's Day when a great number of carriages, people on horseback and foot passengers passed over the bridge. Abraham was awarded the Gold medal from the Royal Society of Arts.

Tontine Hotel

Abraham and his brother, Samuel, together decided to build a nearby hotel in order to generate additional money to pay for the bridge and, at the same time, accommodate visitors to the area. The Tontine Hotel opened in 1784. Such was in the interest in the bridge that stage coaches amended their routes to pass through the Gorge. Trows sailed under the bridge, enabling people to get yet a different view. Visitors included Erasmus Darwin and members of the Lunar Society. Abraham was not unknown to them as he had corresponded with Darwin on scientific subjects. A painting of the Iron Bridge was commissioned from Michael Angelo Rooker, a scene painter at the Haymarket Theatre, London. Engravings were then made and sold to the general public as souvenirs.

Although this was a very exciting period for the family and there was a constant stream of visitors to the bridge and the family home, it has to be remembered that construction of the bridge was both a risky and costly venture. In fact, the Darby family was nearly bankrupted by the costs of building the structure. Abraham's family home, Sunniside, was mortgaged and the sum redeemed was not fully paid off for many years. Abiah lent Abraham £3,000 at 4% interest. He meticulously kept a record of his accounts, paying the interest to her annually.

Following the success of the bridge, other uses were found for cast iron in Shropshire. The Flax Mill in Shrewsbury, is now recognised by World Heritage as the first building in the world to have a cast iron frame. The roof of the picture gallery in Attingham Hall was also recognised as a first.

But suddenly, in the middle of great family success, tragedy occurred.

Abraham and Rebecca's eldest son, Abraham had been sent to live with his grandmother, Abiah, as she lived nearer the school he attended with his cousins. Epidemics at this time were the norm and young Abraham developed 'a putrid fever'. This was scarlet fever! After two days of suffering, the child died - a tremendous blow to the family. He was buried on 9 December 1788.

Sadly, this was only the beginning of a series of disasters. On Christmas Eve, Deborah Darby's father, John Barnard, was taken ill. The family sent for Dr Darwin (Charles Darwin's father) who practiced in Shrewsbury and was renowned for his diagnostic skills. Unfortunately, he told the family there was no hope of the patient's recovery. John died less than three weeks later and was buried in the Friends Burial Ground.

In February, Abraham's brother, Samuel, fell from his horse, but luckily he recovered. Then Abraham III caught scarlet fever. He was very ill, but appeared to make a good recovery. At the same time, his wife Rebecca suffered an extreme sore throat so she was unable to nurse him. Abiah too was ill.

Samuel's wife, Deborah, was fully aware of the dreadful situation, but continued to make plans to go on a Ministry with Rebecca Young. Although she must have had doubts about Samuel's ability to cope in her absence, she left him on 13 March, at a time of great family crisis.

Feeling much better, Abraham felt well enough to go out and ride his horse but unfortunately it was a cold day and this event brought on a relapse. Abraham became seriously ill once more and died on 20 March, aged just 39 years. Abraham III's funeral was held at the Quaker Meeting House and he was buried in the Quaker graveyard.

News reached Deborah of Abraham's death whilst she was in Lancashire, but she did not return home. Her reaction was perhaps not as would be expected for it is reported she said she was 'much distressed on account of the loss ... but did not feel at liberty to go and share it personally with them.' It would appear that Deborah chose not to return to Coalbrookdale when the Darby family were experiencing their worst family crisis. Maybe her own mental state could not cope with the sickness and deaths for she had lost her own father to a stroke only two months before, which must have been a great blow to her. Perhaps she knew Abiah's leadership would carry the close Darby family through this very serious situation.

With the head of the Darby family, the genius behind the making of the Iron Bridge, no longer alive to lead the Coalbrookdale Company, the family and workers at the Ironworks knew they were in deep trouble. Luckily their

Quaker friends, especially the Bristol Iron Masters, offered them important advice, especially how to save the company.

After Abraham III

Following the terrible shock of Abraham's death, Rebecca realised she had been left with little money. No-one had anticipated Abraham's death at such an early age. The making of the bridge had been costly and the Darby family were heavily mortgaged. Abraham had not only used his own money to help fund the building of the bridge, but he had also had to borrow money from Joseph Rathbone and Richard Reynolds to complete the structure. His death had left both Samuel and his family in debt to the Company. Had Abraham lived, the situation would have probably have been different for he would, most likely, have recouped the money.

Abraham and Rebecca had moved into The Haye in 1782, but she soon realised that as a widow, with five young children to bring up and the eldest only 10 years old, she would have to sell the house and its contents. Sale catalogues reveal that the house was very tastefully furnished and perhaps not what would be expected of a Quaker family. They also reveal that Abraham was a man with wide scientific interests.

The library, with an 18 foot square bookcase, contained a large book collection with over 2000 volumes, many beautifully bound in calf skin. Abraham owned a barometer, solar microscopes, a camera obscura, electrical machines, and a weather glass made by Adams of Fleet St in London (instrument makers to George III); objects which were kept in his library. It is known that he had dealings with Erasmus Darwin, who had been one of the first visitors to visit the Iron Bridge. He had also been made a member of the Worshipful Company of Wheelwrights. The catalogue additionally reveals that he was a sportsman for he owned a gun and powder horn, along with a silk net for catching partridges.

The dining room housed the family silver and a Nanking dinner service. The contents included a 19 foot square Wilton carpet, a table and set of mahogany chairs. The chairs in the best parlour were upholstered in silk. The visitors' bedrooms had mahogany furniture with elaborate furnishings. In one bedroom there was a four poster Gothic bedstead, chairs covered in green damask with matching bed and window curtains. The family rooms of the house contained chairs with seats of durable woven hair (probably horse hair). Sadly, all the furniture and possessions had to be sold.

Realising she would be unable to follow her current lifestyle, Rebecca also sold the extensive farmland, stock and various farming implements along with the contents of the house. Abraham had been a great breeder of horses, both for work and pleasure. Strong horses were needed for farm work and for hauling carts of coal and iron at the works. Horses were also used by the family, as a means of travel. Cattle were needed to provide meat, milk and cheese. From now on, the family could only look forward to a much lower standard of living.

Samuel suffered greatly from his brother Abraham's death and the seriousness of his sister Sarah's illness. Deborah's absence too had affected him. She finally returned home on 10 June 1789 to find, 'my beloved husband much indisposed.' In September, Samuel was taken to Shifnal as he became very ill with the return of his nervous mental disorder. In the past his removal from home to different surroundings helped his condition. Deborah visited him at Shifnal and then left on another Ministerial Journey.

Following Abraham III's death, the profitability of the Ironworks declined due to the insecurity of the Darby - Reynolds - Rathbone partnership with Darby family assets mortgaged to both the Rathbones and Reynolds families. Abraham's widow, Rebecca, his sister Sarah and Richard Reynolds were all partners in the company. The Company needed a new Chairman. Sarah realised that her brother Samuel was not the right person for the position (probably due to his mental instability) and refused to elect him as successor. The Coalbrookdale Company needed to survive. However, this was to prove a very difficult time for the quality of the goods declined and their delivery became unreliable.

Abiah

Abiah experienced times of great sadness during her life; family deaths: her first husband and daughter, her second husband Abraham (II) and ultimately their son Abraham (III). However, she was a resilient woman, hardworking, with deep religious beliefs and a strong sense of family. With her husband Abraham's support, Abiah had grown in confidence and found she was able to stand up and speak of her deep religious convictions and so became a Quaker Minister.

During her life at Coalbrookdale, Abiah had a strange friendship with the Rev. Fletcher, Vicar of Madeley. He was of Swiss nationality and was tutor to Thomas Hill of Tern Hill in the 1750s before taking Holy Orders and becoming the Vicar of Madeley in 1760. He and Abiah often enjoyed a battle of words based on their differing beliefs – one discussion lasting some three hours! Neither ever gave way to the other, but their meetings always ended with respectful difference. Quakers refused to pay the compulsory Tithe, an important part of a vicar's income. The Rev. Fletcher was known not to demand Abiah's Tithe payment out of respect for her beliefs, knowing that non-payment could mean a jail sentence. Abiah suggested that the local children needed a Sunday School as there were no day schools to attend. Rev. Fletcher listened. The laying of a foundation stone for this building in 1785 was his last act.

Abiah's health slowly deteriorated and on 26 June 1794 she died at Sunniside, the home she and Abraham had planned and built. She was 78 and her body had slowly declined, but her mind remained clear until her death. She had a peaceful end and was buried in the Quaker graveyard at Coalbrookdale.

There were many testimonies to her good works throughout her lifetime. She was described as:

> a tender sympathiser with the afflicted, whether in body or mind, an eminent example of Christian benevolence of this life, being rich in good works, ready to distribute, willing to communicate, feeding the hungry, clothing the naked, tending the sick and also at sundry times, under special apprehension, of duty, the condemned and other prisoners in different jails.

Abiah had spent most of her life at Coalbrookdale. She was a dominant personality who once she had overcome her inability to speak about spiritual life in public, was able to convince people to lead a more spiritual life themselves. She had lived through great change, seen her son, Abraham III, rise to great fame. She had also experienced great family sorrows. Even today her name is remembered as a strong Quaker lady.

Meanwhile, Deborah had spent three years in North America with Rebecca Young. They had travelled far, crossing land that had only recently been occupied by Europeans. Eventually they returned to Britain in the summer of 1796, to a Coalbrookdale no longer dominated by the presence of Abiah. Deborah records that she was much affected meeting, 'my endeared husband after such a long absence.' During August Samuel became 'indisposed' causing Rebecca to become uneasy. It must have been obvious he was very poorly for Deborah wrote, 'after attending my dearest SD, trying to imagine the awful separation. The "Dear Sufferer" appeared to be passing away with the innocence and sweetness of a Little Child.'

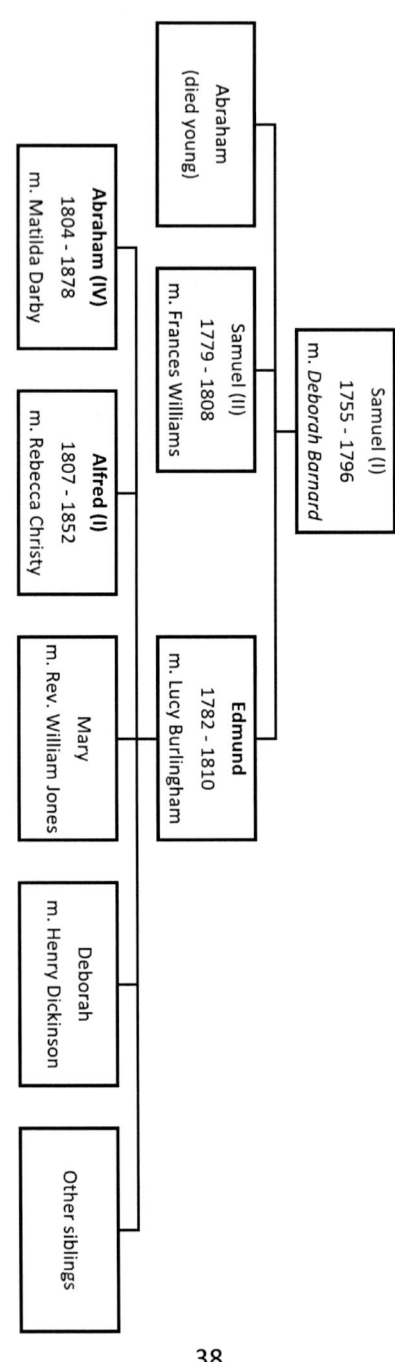

Samuel I and his family

Samuel died at the beginning of September and was buried in the Quaker grave yard. In his will, dated 4 February 1794, Samuel left his company shares in Coalbrookdale and Ketley in Trust to his sisters Mary Rathbone and Sarah Darby for the benefit of his wife and children. Deborah was to be the children's guardian until they reached the age of 21 years. To his son Samuel he left his books, china, plate, linen, household furniture and his wearing apparel.

The dawn of a new century

In 1794 the Darby – Reynolds – Rathbone partnership decided to divide their assets. The Reynolds family took the Ironworks of Ketley and Madeley Wood with the associated mines. The Darby family took Coalbrookdale and Horsehay and importantly kept the right to trade as the Coalbrookdale Company. John Bishton of the Lilleshall Company bought the Donnington Wood blast furnaces. Samuel Darby's son, Edmund, took charge of the Coalbrookdale works and once again bridge building became important. Possibly this was because the Ironbridge over the Severn survived a great flood in 1795 whereas every other bridge had suffered severe damage. Local bridges were replaced and there were orders for bridges in Bristol and overseas in Jamaica. Edmund was supported by his brother, Samuel, and Francis, son of Abraham III. Other active members of the Board were Rebecca (the widow of Abraham III) and Sarah (the daughter of Abraham II).

On 16 September 1801 an explosion occurred when a cloudburst sent a flood of water into the old furnace. The noise broke up a Darby family meeting being held at the works. Everyone rushed out to the scene of devastation. Mary Darby was concerned if there were casualties but miraculously no-one was hurt, but all the buildings had disappeared. Adam Lubbock, a witness at the scene, retold the story of the accident to Randal, a local historian. He commented that, 'Miss Darby was an angel of a woman, as indeed all the Miss Darbys were.' As a result new furnaces had to be built.

On a happier note, Edmund got married in May 1803 to Lucy Burlingham, the daughter of the Worcester businessman to whom he had been apprenticed some years before. Lucy was an attractive girl with deep blue eyes and dark eyelashes. They were married at the Quaker Meeting House in Worcester, before returning to Coalbrookdale.

William Reynolds died in June 1803 and Richard Dearman, manager of the Coalbrookdale Works, died the following year. Change occurred too at Ketley for Joseph Reynolds's brother took over the works.

Following the Darby tradition, Francis Darby (Abraham III's son) should have been made Chairman of the Coalbrookdale Company when he came of age in 1804. But Sarah Darby, his aunt, a formidable lady and the major shareholder in the company, and also Chairman of the shareholders, opposed this suggestion. She did not consider him suitable for the position, possibly because he had an unpredictable and at times a very unstable temper.

In 1806, a Tax was threatened on pig iron, which could have affected sales, as there was already a keen price-war. This could have proved a difficult problem for the Coalbrookdale management. However, Edmund was imaginative and dynamic and his management ensured the future of the Ironworks, making the company increasingly secure.

Family Tragedy: Edmund, Samuel II and Deborah's later life

Family life did not run smoothly, for Edmund's brother, Samuel, started to associate and make friends with individuals who were not of the Quaker religion. To add to this he even told his mother Deborah that he wished join the army. This was totally against Quaker beliefs. One wonders whether his friendship with Frances Williams of Welshpool, who came from a Church of England family and who he later married, was the cause of this change. Having been left company shares by his father, Samuel was not dependent on his mother. He bought a house at Berwick, on the northern outskirts of Shrewsbury.

Surprisingly, Deborah did not mention this personal upheaval in her diary. Nor does she mention the birth of a daughter, Frances, at Sunniside, in 1806, described as a beautiful child. Sadly the child became ill and died in 1811. She was buried in Welshpool. It would appear Samuel's wife Frances wasn't accepted into the family, although her daughter was born at Sunniside.

Many years later, Adelaide, the fourth diarist, recorded being taken by her father Francis to Welshpool where they stayed at the Royal Oak Hotel. Francis took her to the churchyard where she was shown a memorial: 'In Sacred Memory of Frances Ann aged 7 years died 1811. Here lies the grief of a fond mother.' The fond mother was Frances Darby, by now, Samuel's widow. Later that day, the Williams family home was pointed out to her. Although Adelaide recorded the visit, she made no mention of the family relationship.

When Samuel left the Quaker fold, Deborah did not disown or desert her son. Soon afterwards, he began suffering from violent nosebleeds and his health deteriorated. Deborah began visiting him at his house at Berwick. After one visit she wrote, 'My beloved child … appears in a declining state of health.' Samuel died on 1 February 1808. His mother wrote, 'Samuel, my endeared child, sweetly departed this life about 2am this morning, having been mercifully cared for, so we may say the Lord's Mercy are new every morning.'

On 6 February his body was taken to Dale House, just as his great grandfather, Abraham I's, had been, and he was buried the following day. After his funeral, his mother ministered to the people. A witness remarked, 'Samuel in some measure, perhaps, has been accepted back into the fold.' Perhaps his wife, Frances, wished to give her mother-in-law some small consolation by allowing him a Quaker funeral and burial. Frances gave birth to a second daughter, Mary, after Samuel's death. One wonders whether Samuel was the first member of the Darby family to desert the Quaker faith?

Deborah was a true Christian and never wavered in her beliefs. Both her husband and son caused her great unhappiness. Her husband's instability and the loss of a thriving business caused her great concern. Then to have, what was considered at the time, a wayward son, must have been devastating. She was a forgiving and loving mother who supported him through his last illness. Although he had left the Quaker faith, she forgave him, and brought his body home and buried him with his Darby ancestors.

Deborah Darby died in February 1810 with her son Edmund at her side. She had lived for 56 years, putting the 'Word of God' before everything she did. She had travelled all over the British Isles and North America preaching to those of the Quaker faith. Often she visited prisons. What is truly remarkable is that she is still remembered to this day for her Quaker Ministry and prison reform. Often referred to as 'Dear Deborah Darby', a member of the Friends community wrote during her life:

> She is of a gentle nature, not at all aggressive in her speeches and commitment. Neither does she care about being fashionable. Comfort and durability is all she needs.

A facet also borne out by James Jenkins, a London Quaker stockbroker, when he wrote:

> Although getting out of fashion with even our plainest woman friends, she retained the beaver hat so generally worn by Quaker females in the days of my youth.

He went on to say:

> Her voice was sweet and harmonious. She expressed herself in short sentences, every one of which had a tuneful termination. She was a woman of fine person; in her air and aspect dignity was mingled with sweetness, for I have heard from those who knew her much better than myself, that in the disposition of her mind conscious elevation of sentiment was softened by mild and other amiable affections.

Her only fault was that she seemed to be unable to face certain situations. Her husband Samuel's mental condition is one thing she appears to ignore. Maybe she felt her own mental stability would falter if she was left to cope.

Tragedy continued and fate intervened once more as it often did throughout the Darby dynasty. In June of the same year, Edmund decided to go to a relative's wedding in Melksham, Wiltshire. It was a great shock to everyone when he developed food poisoning and subsequently died. Like the other Darby widows before her, Lucy, was left with five small children to bring up and would have to show great strength and resolution.

The Coalbrookdale Management now had to find a suitable successor to Edmund. After leaving school, Francis was in line to take over the

Coalbrookdale works. His aunt, Sarah Darby, was the largest shareholder in the Company, but she would not agree to Francis taking over. Francis was known to have an unpredictable temper which she feared might surface and sour relations with prospective customers and day-to-day dealings with the workforce. Instead Sarah suggested Barnard Dickinson as Edmund's successor. His mother was a Darby and so was his wife, but he knew nothing about running an Ironworks. He had been trained in agriculture and horse breeding and was used to managing the large Darby estates. He was plucked from his farming background and put in charge of the Darby Ironworks which must have been a great shock to him. He was a conscientious man but despite this, the Ironworks began to stagnate for the products lacked flair and new ideas. This situation persisted until the Darby brothers, Abraham IV and Alfred took over the management of the Ironworks in 1830.

Francis Darby and his family (Hannah, Matilda and Adelaide)

As she grew older, Francis often accompanied his Aunt Deborah on her Ministry. It was on one of these journeys, when they travelled to Leighton Buzzard, that he met his future wife, Hannah Grant. She was the daughter of John and Hannah Grant. Deborah approached the parents proposing her nephew Francis as a suitable son-in-law. He was accepted and a special meeting was called at Hogsty End where they announced their intention to marry. They were married on 11 May 1808.

A number of years later, in 1817, Francis visited Parkgate on the Wirral peninsula. After bathing in the sea, he became extremely ill. It is thought that Francis may have suffered a brain haemorrhage. He was taken by his father-in-law John Grant to Leighton Buzzard to convalesce. Here Francis and Hannah rented a house called Linslade. They lived here for a year, during which time, Francis made a full recovery. One cannot be sure whether this episode affected his position and career in the Coalbrookdale

Company, but naturally artistic he was able to bring these skills to fruition once the Company was being run by Alfred and Abraham. The Ironwork's accounts show that both Francis and Abraham received salaries over a four year period, totaling over £47,000!

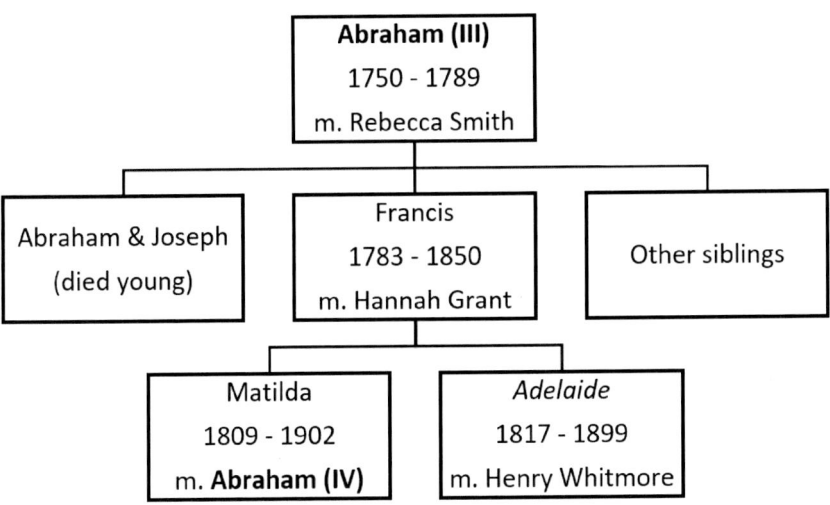

Darby family tree showing Abraham III and Francis (diarist shown in italics)

As a result, Francis could afford expensive continental holidays for his family and was able to expand his landholdings in Coalbrookdale. He began extending his ownership of property of land and houses in the neighbourhood of Sunniside. In 1816 he bought Furnace Bank Farm which adjoined the White House and then land known as 'The Whales Back' and a further 70 acres of land originally belonging to Richard Reynolds. He bought property to gain the freeholds and began to demolish the smaller houses. By 1841, Francis was the largest landholder in the Dale. The only houses remaining were belonging to Dr Edwards, their family doctor, and his son. In order to display his wealth, Francis purchased a coach on which he displayed the Darby coat of arms. However, the right to this was disputed by the Court of Heralds! Coach houses and stables for the horses were built in an attempt to further improve his status in the community. Francis also became a collector of fine porcelain and silver – and again these were decorated with the Darby coat of arms. Books were purchased, but in pride of place, occupying three rooms, was his collection of expensive paintings. Francis had become a man of substance in the local community.

Francis and Hannah had two daughters, Matilda, born in 1809, and Adelaide, born in 1817. Although they were born eight years apart, they got on extremely well together. Their parents ensured that both girls were well educated. Unlike former generations, they were educated at home with visiting tutors and governesses. They travelled extensively during their lives, not for the Quaker cause like their predecessors, but purely for their education and enjoyment. Adelaide was a bright girl, forward and serious for her age. When she reached the age of 16 she was given Dr Walker's Dictionary, by her father. She decided on receiving this adult book, to remove from her bookshelves all the books she had enjoyed reading in her childhood. Her Grandfather Grant was extremely generous and gave her £20, about £1,000 in today's money. She made a resolution to keep a journal and wrote rather pompously that it would be 'an account of progressive mental improvement.' At first she recorded the books she read, walks and outings. Gradually she wrote about her family and the people she met. Then came thoughts of marriage and probable suitors. Being an eligible girl there were many. So many in fact, her father rejected some without consulting her. She too rejected out of hand. In her journal, which she kept until 1861, she revealed her innermost thoughts, making some very cryptic comments about suitors, her family and people in general. Unlike the previous diaries, written by her ancestors Abiah and Deborah, Adelaide wrote very little about Quaker Meetings, her faith, or the Coalbrookdale Ironworks - the foundation of her family's wealth. She enjoyed a good social life and made lists of important people and places she visited. She gave first-hand accounts of royal events, parliamentary debates, exhibitions and being entertained by the rich and powerful. As such her writings are in complete contrast to the earlier diaries.

By the 1830s, Rebecca Darby, mother of Francis and widow of Abraham III, had become frail, so she lived with Francis and his family. She had been widowed early in life and had educated and brought up five children. In June 1834, Adelaide planned a party for the extended Darby family on the Wrekin. Although Rebecca was unwell, plans for the party went ahead. The outing proved enjoyable, but on reaching the bottom of the Wrekin, a messenger was waiting with an envelope sealed with black wax. Rebecca had died. She had reached the age of 82, dying 55 years after her husband. Adelaide does not mention anything in her diary about the funeral or burial, which was probably in the Quaker graveyard.

A new era – Abraham IV and Alfred

Abraham and his brother Alfred took over the running of the Coalbrookdale Ironworks in 1830. They had studied the working of the company and were not impressed with the workmanship of the goods produced, or the attitude of the workforce. Their first act was to reduce costs. The large steam engines, used by the Company were fuelled with high quality coals. Slack, a much cheaper fuel was substituted - a change which proved very successful. The engines used 600 - 700 tons less fuel per week than previously. Not only was money saved but the slack also reduced the sulphurous fumes which had filled the valley.

Next, they set out to improve working standards. The quality of workmanship had fallen due to lack of supervision and leadership. The brothers set a good example by being early to work, staying on the site late and being visible at unexpected hours. These actions were not popular with the workforce but gradually there was an improvement in production and of the quality of the products. The brothers could now concentrate on their new ideas and this is where Francis's help became invaluable.

A Bristol Ironworks had decided to build a revolutionary iron ship. Plates and boilers were needed and the Darbys were asked to produce them. As a result the Coalbrookdale Company built a new port on the Severn for boats to dock and a large warehouse for storing the goods. In addition, a new plate-way was constructed to bring the goods down to the warehouse. The Horsehay works rolled the plates. The iron ship being built at Bristol was named 'The Great Britain'. It was successful, a completely new material being used in the ship building industry.

Matilda, fell in love with her cousin, Abraham Darby. He had inherited the deep blue eyes of his mother, Lucy Burlingham. Matilda called him, 'the sunshine of her world.' They became engaged on Christmas Day 1838 and were married at the Coalbrookdale Meeting House on the 8 August 1839. Although it was wet, the ride to the ceremony did not put off the many spectators. They waved handkerchiefs and threw roses into the carriage. The wedding procession passed under many banners and arches of brightly coloured flowers along the route. One of these had the bride and groom's intertwined initials and proclaimed, 'Prosperity to the House of Darby.' Cannon were fired, making this a triumphal ride to and from the Meeting House. There were four bridesmaids accompanying Matilda, her sister Adelaide being the chief one. The bride was in white with a bonnet and scarf. Following the ceremony they all adjourned to the new Severn warehouse which was well decorated. Adelaide described the wedding breakfast as, 'the dejeuner a la couchette, which was elegant in the extreme.' It was a very popular marriage and reception.

After the reception the bridal party left for the station, Adelaide accompanying her sister on the honeymoon. This was common practice at this time. Throngs of people lined Lincoln Hill to the station. Here they caught a train to Birmingham, staying the night at the new Royal Hotel. The next day they travelled to London to catch a train to Southampton, where they were to spend their honeymoon. They left the train, supposedly at Southampton, and Abraham ordered to be taken to an inn. They unpacked and dressed for dinner, Adelaide helping Matilda. There was a knock on the door; it was Abraham and Adelaide went to speak to him. He broke the news that unfortunately they were in Winchester and not Southampton! Abraham, amid great laughter, had to tell the Innkeeper their mistake. While everything was repacked, they visited the Cathedral and city and were very impressed. By 6 o'clock everything was repacked and they were well pleased with Abraham's blunder, enjoying Winchester and the ride to Southampton. Here they stayed at the Dolphin Hotel; Adelaide and Abraham walking on the beach and pier, considering it a beautiful place. Abraham remarked that 'if they knew of our adventures at home they would give me a certificate for the lunatic asylum!'

Following the Company's expansion in Liverpool during 1844, Adelaide, Abraham and Matilda were invited to the city to launch a new merchant ship built of iron. They were met and escorted by Henry Darby, who ran the Liverpool Ironworks. The next day a great many people arrived for the ceremony. The spectators stood on the deck of another unfinished vessel whilst Mr Blain escorted Matilda to the launching platform, where the bottle of champagne was attached to the figure head. It was a windy day and Matilda had great difficulty swinging the champagne bottle. The mate assisted with a helpful tug and the ship was duly christened the 'Robert Cobden.' The ship slid with a thunderous lurch into the sea. Following this excitement the large party of 200 people, many of them Liverpool aristocracy, moved from the viewing platform to enjoy a fine lunch. Afterwards, Abraham IV, gave a speech on Free Trade.

With Abraham and Alfred leading the Company, Francis's artistic talents began to surface. He was well travelled both in Britain and on the continent and these experiences helped him to bring fresh, new ideas to Coalbrookdale. It was during this period that the works became renowned for its decorative ironwork.

In May 1845 the Anti-Corn Law League held a bazaar in London. Abraham IV was a strong supporter of the League and agreed to display some of Coalbrookdale's recent work. For the first time their new cast iron products were shown to the general public. These included statues of prominent men, including Goethe, Napoleon, Wellington and Benjamin Franklin. Catalogues listed the great range of goods produced at this time, items of pure art to machinery and steam engines.

Abraham's brother Alfred was attracted to Adelaide but she did not return his feelings. He was persistent in his advances for some time but in October 1846, after yet another proposal of marriage, she finally rejected him. Alfred finally realised his quest for Adelaide's hand in marriage was hopeless. However, it was not long before Rebecca Christy caught Alfred's attention as a suitable bride! The Christy family were a rich, prominent Quaker family of bankers, hatters and cotton manufacturers - the first manufacturers of Turkish towelling in Britain. They had exhibited at the Anti-Corn Law League bazaar; during which time the two families had become friendly.

Adelaide noticed Alfred's interest in Rebecca and a latent jealousy surfaced. She was obviously loathed to lose Alfred's adoration and attention, and made a number of cutting and unkind remarks: 'I am afraid if that poor girl marries him, she marries misery' and 'No doubt she will have him, his proposal is under consideration.' She continued 'Alfred Darby is really accepted - I believe half married. It will be an agreeable fact that people cannot say I am to marry him' and 'I thought he looked happy. I do not see why she should make him so.'

Alfred and Rebecca were married in 1848 at the Quaker Meeting house in Kingston upon Thames in London. Alfred was 41, Rebecca 27. Abraham and Matilda were invited to the wedding but Adelaide did not attend. Adelaide commented that Matilda wore a very elegant dress but described the wedding as a 'vulgar affair.' She did not write anything more! Alfred and Rebecca settled in 'Bromfield,' a pleasant house on Clapham Common. Adelaide received an invitation to visit and naturally her curiosity compelled her to accept their invitation!

Alfred, along with Abraham and Francis, were all interested in the Arts, spending their fortune on paintings, china and books. The brothers, now both married, started looking for suitable Shropshire properties that could house their growing collections.   Alfred wished to move back to the Coalbrookdale area to be closer to the Ironworks. Stanley House at Astley Abbots near Bridgnorth became available. While Abraham was considering renting the property, Alfred stepped in and was accepted as tenant!

Alfred and Rebecca moved into Stanley House and settled down to married life. On 7 September 1850 a son and heir, Alfred Edmund William Darby, was born. There was great rejoicing and festivities in Coalbrookdale; the employees were given pink and white scarves which they waved enthusiastically and followed in a procession, led by a dwarf on horseback. There were a number of brass bands and banners. The last in this procession was employee, William Ball, who weighed 40 stone. To sit on his horse he was hoisted upwards by a crane! After all this noisy marching a feast had been prepared. The Darby farms produced 1,700 loaves of bread and 1,000 gallons of ale. The meat for the meal was home produced: nine bullocks and 40 sheep were cooked for the feast. The women and children were entertained at a tea party for 1,000. The Managerial Staff had a dinner, followed by a grand ball. Alfred II's birth would be long remembered.

The following year Alice Mary was born and soon afterwards Rebecca was pregnant again.

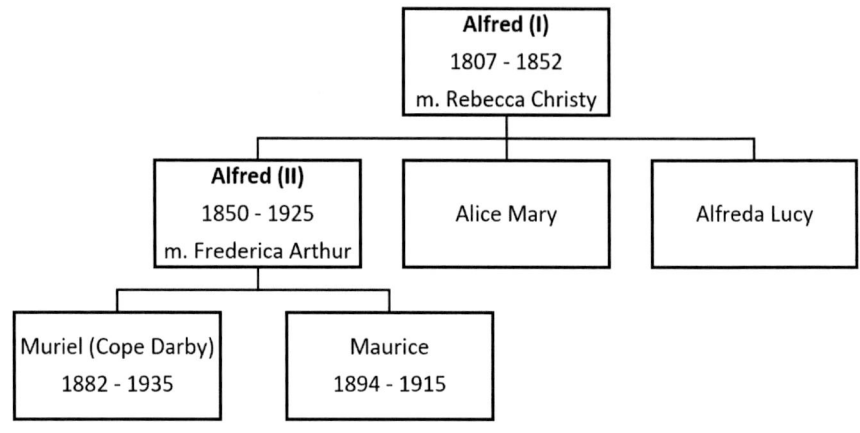

Family tree showing Alfred I and II

When Adelaide was invited to a ball at Stanley House in March 1851, she wrote:

> Magnificent rooms and supper and chandeliers. The Grand Piano was in the entrance hall supported by violins and flute. I do not think the affair was badly done, nor that it gave as much pleasure as might have been expected from so much expenditure.

Adelaide, it seemed, could only ever give Alfred and Rebecca faint praise!

The younger generation leave the Quaker fold

On one occasion, after a bout of illness, Matilda was taken by Abraham and Adelaide to Bath to recuperate. Whilst staying in the area they attended Church of England services, at Bath Abbey and Gloucester Cathedral. On returning to Coalbrookdale they began attending services in Little Wenlock Church where they became friendly with the curate, C.H. Hartshorne. Abraham and Matilda enjoyed the services and were baptised into the Church of England on 22 August 1849.

Now that the younger members of the Darby family had turned towards the Church of England, they decided to build a church in Ironbridge. Adelaide gave one and a half acres of land on the farm she owned and made a public footpath across the field to the church. Alfred had bought a field which turned out to have very good brick clay. He started a brick making yard and donated the bricks for the new building. He also donated the metal tracery around the window which was made at the Coalbrookdale works with malleable cast iron. Mary Darby, sister of Abraham and Alfred, gave a peal of bells. It was a Darby family church.

The foundation stone was to be officially laid by Mr Henry Whitmore on 24 November 1851. Adelaide had specially requested the event should not happen this week, as it was inconvenient for her. When she asked Dr Marshall, who was in charge, why he had gone against her wishes, he replied that this week was more convenient for Mrs Alfred Darby! This was obviously not very tactful. On completion of the church building a Dedicational Service was arranged. There was a large gathering of clergymen at Sunniside the day before the Dedication. (How the old Quaker house, Sunniside, must have shivered to see a large gathering representing the Church of England!) There was some confusion when the Archdeacon lost his gown but luckily it was retrieved by midnight and he was able to wear it for the service.

Holy Trinity Church, Coalbrookdale

Francis's will and a family split

In 1848, Francis sent for the family solicitor, Mr Potts from Broseley, to draw up his will. However, when it was drawn up, he refused to sign it. Instead he just asked for his bill! His explanation being, 'the law would make a better will for him, than he could do himself,' meaning, his estate and possessions would be divided equally between his daughters. However, due to his wife's actions, this did not actually take place. Under the terms of the will, Adelaide was to be the principal beneficiary and Francis's wife, Hannah, was to have the household furniture, plate, linen, books, pictures, horses, carriages and all other effects. Francis made a number of generous bequests to his staff: to his gardener, John Paston, £200; William Morris, labourer, £50; John Hanley, labourer, £50; Henry Davies, footman, £200, a good ring with garnet, gold repeating watch, all his clothes, boots and shoes of all descriptions, in remembrance of his services to him, provided he was living with him when he died; to Margaret Webb, housemaid, £50. All the servants living with him on his death were to be given a years' wages. To his nephew, Joseph Dickinson, he left £100 and £30 to poor old Amelia Edwards. All money for debts and all affects were bequeathed to his son-in-law, Abraham Darby and his nephew, Alfred Darby, in Trust to pay his funeral expenses and legacies.

When Francis died in 1850, his wife Hannah showed an unwillingness to follow the instructions of her husband's unsigned will. Adelaide was not happy, as her father dying intestate meant she would probably not be as rich as she had hoped and therefore would only attract 'second class gentry' in marriage. Matilda had expected to inherit Sunniside and Adelaide the Hay Estate. Sunniside had been empty for 30 years; it was a large and prestigious house which would have fitted Abraham's status as manager of the Coalbrookdale Company. Hannah however implied that Matilda and Abraham would continue to live in the White House.

After her father's death, Matilda felt free to write about her family. She records that her husband, Abraham, was summoned by telegraph to return to Coalbrookdale to arrange Francis's funeral. He wrote letters and gave orders for the funeral. Matilda reports that Adelaide was in a state of excitement and did not appear grief stricken at the death of her father, although she was reported as saying, she was 'desolate at the death of the Head of the family.' Matilda added that this was inconsistent with the bitter and slighting tone which she used to speak of her father. In the event, Hannah, Matilda and Adelaide were unable to attend the funeral because of deep snow.

It has been suggested that Matilda and Adelaide had an idyllic childhood. This was not always true, for Matilda says her father Francis had a violent temper, even when healthy. From childhood she had a sense of fear, and reserve on his part made for an unhappy childhood. At one point Francis was obsessed with the belief his wife was having an affair and he spoke of this to family and friends. His behaviour was such that many close family friends began to worry for Hannah's safety. Adelaide too was subjected to her father's unreasonable behaviour. He accused her of impropriety and made unpleasant scenes. Adelaide seriously considered leaving home at one stage but Matilda and Abraham advised her strongly against this idea for they realised she would not be able to earn a living to support herself.

Ultimately, Matilda decided not to contest the will; she withdrew her objections and Abraham and Matilda decided to leave the Dale. They travelled to the Home Counties to view suitable estates and eventually settled on Stoke Court in Buckinghamshire. The house had been built by the Quaker Penn family who had emigrated to North America and founded the district of Pennsylvania. By February 1851, Abraham and Matilda had purchased the estate and on Thursday 10 April Adelaide wrote in her diary, 'Matilda left us today.' Her entry for that day concluded: 'Great was the change from past days that they should both go without word of invitation - Abraham without ever saying goodbye or I shall hope to see you.'

The workforce and inhabitants of the Dale were horrified at this turn of events as Abraham had been an excellent employer.

The Great Exhibition

Prince Albert was an ardent supporter of industrialisation and wished to place Great Britain as the world leader of manufactured goods. He came up with the idea of a Great Exhibition to show the world the quality and uniqueness of British manufactured goods. This challenge was exactly what the Coalbrookdale Company needed and, before his untimely death, Francis produced innovative designs for decorative ironwork. The first exhibits at the exhibition were four ornamental bronzed cast iron gates. Each gate was cast in one single piece. The gates can still be seen at the entrance to Kensington Gardens. The second huge construction was a rustic dome made in cast iron, 30 feet high and 20 feet in diameter. There were six double pillars with finials of guarding falcons with a statuette of Aeolus. Inside, there was a casting of 'The Eagle Slayer' which was 11.5 feet high. The eagle was transfixed by an arrow of the archer. Another casting was a fountain, 7 feet wide and 8 feet high of Cupid and the Swan. Today this can be seen at Coalbrookdale. A casting of Andromeda was purchased by Queen Victoria and is at Osborne House on the Isle of Wight. The Great Exhibition showed Coalbrookdale as one of the World's foremost Ironworks.

Statue of Andromeda, now at Osbourne House, Isle of Wight
(reproduced by kind permission of The Stoke Poges Society)

As well as these large pieces, the Company also made smaller garden furniture and household articles. Previously made in wood, these were now made in cast iron. Their stoves and fireplaces were the basis for today's Aga and Rayburn cookers; still popular in country households today, over 160 years later. 1851 proved to be the pinnacle of Darby design and production. Coalbrookdale was the largest iron foundry in the world, producing outstanding metal goods. As with Abraham III and the Ironbridge, Francis sadly did not live to see or receive his full acclaim for he died in 1850 before the opening of the Exhibition.

A sense of the popularity and grandeur of the Great Exhibition is revealed in Adelaide's diary:

> We set out at about half past 8 and were informed there had been a double line of carriages from 5 o'clock the whole length of Piccadilly to the Exhibition! So with much difficulty got to the Albert Gate and walked from there. The first entrance to the Building was most grand and imposing – from North to South a third of a mile in length and filled with the most magnificent statues and foundations and then the Queen's throne with its blue and gold canopy.

At 1.30pm the Queen arrived and the exhibition was officially opened. Adelaide goes on to describe the royal party:

> The Queen pink and silver brocade and diamonds. She had the little Prince of Wales with her in Highland costume. Prince Albert in Full Military uniform, the Princess Royal is very plain. She had

a wreath of wild roses very like a ballet dancer and a lace dress.

Adelaide visited the Exhibition a number of times and on the 8 May wrote 'We go tomorrow to Stoke Court.' Adelaide was impressed with Matilda's new home, writing, 'Stoke Court is the sweetest place in the world and the most beautifully furnished.' The healing process between the two sisters had begun!

Stoke Court
(reproduced by kind permission of The Stoke Poges Society)

Adelaide's marriage

Throughout her adult life Adelaide had innumerable proposals of marriage. She was now 35 years of age and considered herself 'on the shelf.' Her only consolation was that on inheriting most of her father's wealth she would have a comfortable old age. She was apparently upset at the departure of Abraham and Matilda to Stoke Court but in no way did she blame herself for their departure.

The local community realised she was now a wealthy woman and during 1851 she was invited to Dudmaston to stay with the Whitmore family. This visit worried her more than a previous visit to Willey to stay with the Forrester family, for she realised that she was being inspected by the upper gentry as a prospective bride. Henry Whitmore of Apley Park, a bachelor and third son, was one of the guests. His eldest brother, Thomas, lived in the family home and was married to Lady Louisa Douglas. His second brother, George, was Rector of Stockton. As a third son, Henry did not have great wealth or prospects. He wished to become an MP, but as they did not receive a salary, a large fortune was necessary. It was obvious that Adelaide was being seriously considered by the family as an eligible bride. After the visit, Adelaide was taken by various Whitmore ladies to a number of local events. She must have impressed them for she proved she was acceptable to join the family and be a suitable wife for Henry. She was well educated, well-travelled, and most importantly she had a sizeable fortune.

Hannah Darby, her mother, was approached by Henry and asked for permission to propose to Adelaide. This was obviously an ideal arrangement for both Adelaide and Henry. After a few days she replied accepting Henry's proposal. As Henry's wife she would be accepted by the very cream of Shropshire Society. The marriage was arranged for 15 April 1852 in the church in Coalbrookdale, which she and other members of the Darby family had planned, built and endowed. On her wedding day she wrote in her journal the words, 'I was married.' The honeymoon was in Malvern.

As with previous Darbys, tragedy took over. A message was brought from Stanley House, to Adelaide's wedding that Alfred had died, leaving his wife, Rebecca, with two small children and expecting a third. Alfred had died from erysipelas, a virulent and very painful skin infection, from which there were few survivors. Yet another Darby in his prime had died leaving a young widow.

Adelaide reveals in her journal that Rebecca coped very well with widowhood. As with previous Darby wives, she showed strong character and coped remarkably with her new place in Society. Adelaide remained friendly with Rebecca and records a number of visits to Stanley House. In 1857, she was invited to help Rebecca organize a bazaar in the grounds of the Hall. Adelaide records that the event was held in a long tent, was well attended and made a profit of £300.

When he was old enough, Rebecca's son, Alfred II was enrolled at Eton and on leaving school joined Merton College, Oxford. With no father figure, Rebecca's unmarried brothers, Alexander and Edmund (Christy), played a great part in his early life. And, it was probably through his erudite uncles, Edmund - Uncle 'Teddy' and Alexander - Uncle 'Mog,' that Alfred learnt to appreciate the fine arts. Alfred was brought up to be a country gentleman, developing a great interest in agriculture, horse breeding and country sports: shooting, fishing and riding.

The Shropshire Bank

Abraham IV and his cousin Henry Dickinson together owned the Shropshire Bank. At this time there were no national banks; instead they were run by local families. Although Abraham and Matilda had moved away from the Dale, Abraham remained a proprietor of the Bank. Early one morning, in November 1854, Henry Dickinson, who had married Deborah Darby, arrived at Stoke Court with devastating news. He had received an unexpected visit from Mr Allen, the Wellington Branch Manager who told him he had speculated with the Bank's money (a sum equivalent to £8,000,000 today), and had lost it all! As proprietors, Abraham and Henry were responsible for every last penny. The utmost secrecy was needed. Other than some bank officials, only Deborah and Matilda, were told. The public was unaware of the situation. A Mr Foster gave notice that he would be withdrawing £30,000. Surprisingly, this transaction took place without any problems!

Matilda's sister Adelaide was unaware of the crisis. She did however make reference to a comment of Matilda's in her journal in December 1857, when writing that she had visited Stoke Court with her mother and found Matilda and Abraham suffering from influenza. She noted that 'they said they were in trouble and were coming to poverty.' Matilda had lost out on her father's will and Abraham, through no fault of his own, was in great monetary trouble.

In order to pay depositors such as Mr Foster and ultimately save the Bank, Abraham sold his valuable collection of paintings and books. Then he sold Stoke Court, his Buckinghamshire retirement home. It seems probable that the sale of Abraham and Matilda's home and their associated assets covered his share of the Bank's losses. Henry meanwhile sold his estate in Little Ness. Together these actions saved the bank and it is to their credit that no one else became involved or lost their savings. The Shropshire Bank was eventually bought by Lloyds in 1874.

The final Iron Master and the end of an era.

Having sold Stoke Court, Abraham needed to work. He and Matilda moved to South Wales in 1861 where he became Managing Director of the Ebbw Vale Steel, Iron and Coal Company. Under Abraham's direction the Works prospered and became a larger enterprise than the Coalbrookdale Company! Abraham retired in 1873 having sold the Company's patents to the Bessemer Company for £80,000 some years earlier. Abraham and Matilda did not return to Coalbrookdale but moved to Llangorse Lake near Brecon. Abraham was the last of the Coalbrookdale Iron Masters. When he died in 1878 his body was taken by train for burial at Holy Trinity Church, which he had helped build many years before. The road from Coalbrookdale station to the church was lined with local people showing their respect for the Darby family.

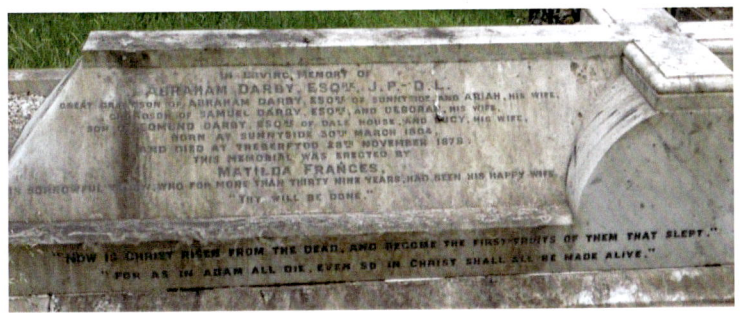

Abraham IV and Matilda's tombstone, Holy Trinity Church

In 1888, at the age of 71, Adelaide made her will leaving her sister Matilda the Sunniside estate and Greenbank Farm. Adelaide died in 1899, and at the age of 91, Matilda moved back to Sunniside, her birthplace, which she should have inherited almost 50 years earlier. By now she was the only one alive to enjoy it. Matilda died on 16 December 1902, aged 93. On her death, the last of the Coalbrookdale estates passed to her nephew, Alfred II.

An initial link with Baschurch parish

Abraham IV's sister, Mary, was known as 'Queen of the Dales'. As she was unmarried, her brother advised her to buy some land in Baschurch parish in north Shropshire, which the Duke of Cleveland was selling. Taking her brother's advice, she purchased land in Fenemere and Eyton. Like other younger members of the Darby family in the mid nineteenth century, she also converted to the Church of England, and on October 27 1858 married the Rev. William Jones who was vicar of Baschurch. The wedding took place at Abraham's family home, Stoke Court. The Rev. Jones was a widower with a daughter from his first marriage, and owned an estate in Pontesbury.

Henry Dickinson, Deborah Darby and a move to Little Ness

Henry Dickinson, joint owner of the Shropshire Bank with Abraham IV, was an agriculturalist like his father Barnard. He had married Deborah Darby

(Abraham and Alfred's sister) in 1841. In 1850, the Earl of Powis decided to sell his land in Little Ness in Baschurch parish - an area not unknown to the Darby family - and Henry decided to purchase the estate. There were a number of farm houses on the estate but no major house, or any important landowning family living in the township. Little Ness had a small chapel built on the bailey of a small Norman castle. There were views of the south Shropshire Hills, the Wrekin and the Welsh Hills. The surrounding agricultural land was of excellent quality and well known in Shropshire for its productivity.

Henry enlarged and renovated one of the farmhouses in the area near the church making it an attractive small country house. Deborah obviously enjoyed their Little Ness estate as she was staying there when taken very ill in the autumn of 1855. A number of doctors attended Deborah but sadly they could not help. Members of the family came to the house. Adelaide wrote:

> To our horror this evening, Mrs Henry Dickinson died this morning at Ness. We knew that she was ill of inflammation of the bowels. They went last Wednesday, with Mrs Edmund Darby and Mary to spend a day at Ness and the spasms she had before, came on that evening. R Thursfield and four other doctors were in attendance. Her funeral was on 3 November.

The Coalbrookdale Works were closed as a mark of respect. Deborah's death must have compounded the shock Henry had received the previous November about the Shropshire Bank. In the years that followed, Henry remarried (Susanna Hadwen from Liverpool) and bought additional land adjoining the estate. This was located on the Ruyton-XI-Towns border - an area known as Queen's Court and Five Ways, plus a section of the Cliffe - a sandstone outcrop with a working quarry. The area was good for rough shooting. By 1863 Henry's Little Ness estate amounted to 1,012 acres.

Rebecca and Alfred II move to Little Ness

When Rebecca discovered that the owners of Stanley Hall would not renew her lease, she had a choice: find another suitable house to rent or build her own house which Alfred could inherit. Great decisions were made by Rebecca and her Christy brothers. They decided to build their own country mansion and their thoughts, possibly influenced by Henry Dickinson's financial situation, turned to Baschurch parish. Rebecca purchased the Little Ness estate from Henry Dickinson in 1868 and in 1873 Alfred II inherited Mary Jones's (neé Darby) land in Fenemere and Eyton. These two estates would make a large estate for Rebecca and her son, and, the perfect setting for a new country house. The ideal solution!

Building of Adcote

Following the purchase of the Little Ness estate by Rebecca Darby, Alexander Christy invited the architect Norman Shaw to visit the site and produce suitable designs for a country house. The house would not follow any particular style, it was to be a mixture of Medieval, Tudor, William Morris and Art Nouveau. The site chosen was an old farmhouse in the hamlet of Adcote. There were clear views in every direction: the South Shropshire Hills, the Long Mynd, Long Mountain and the Breiden Hills, beautifully silhouetted on the horizon - the perfect situation for a country house.

When Henry Dickinson re-built Little Ness Farm, he had used sandstone from a local quarry, situated on Red House Farm. To take the stone from the quarry to Adcote would not be difficult, as the Darby Company often used horse-drawn tramways for conveying raw materials and completed products around their sites. The contract for building the house was awarded to Hale and Sons of Salisbury. The initial sum quoted was £16,455 although the final sum was nearly twice that figure, £29,792. The interior needed a modern decorator and J Adam Heaton was engaged.

Shaw was a popular architect and while supervising the building of Adcote, he was also engaged in the construction of four other houses. With this heavy workload he was taken ill. He kept in touch, but made few visits. The estimated length of construction was two years, but this overran. Shaw submitted his Adcote designs to the Royal Academy of Arts and was awarded a Diploma. He was also elected as a member of the Royal Academy. A view of Adcote was hung in the gallery at Burlington House. This must have been very pleasing to Rebecca Darby and her Christy brothers.

Adcote

The heart of the house was the Great Hall. This followed the medieval style, with a huge fireplace dominating the room. One end of the room had a double gallery and on the south wall, at the opposite end, there was a large oriel window. This room was designed to entertain and impress.

Coalbrookdale fireplaces and grates were used throughout the house and both the Jackfield and the Maw Company produced beautifully designed coloured tiles. Coalport china was bought for use by the family. William Morris wallpapers were hung in the bedrooms and many of these rooms still carry the original names: Fern, Carnation and Hollyhock.

The grounds reflected the beauty of the house. A Christy ancestor had been a distinguished Royal Gardener at Holyrood House. Country houses of this period had large kitchen gardens to provide the vegetables, fruit and flowers needed for the household. There were eight gardeners, three for the walled garden, two in the heated greenhouses producing grapes and peaches, and three working in the grounds. Rebecca Darby brought the head gardener with her from Astley Abbots. The younger men were housed in a bothy and houses were built for the older workers.

Stable Block, Adcote

The Darbys had a love of horses and a stable block was constructed with a clock tower containing a chiming clock. There were six to seven horses in the stables with a coachman, grooms and stable boys; a brougham, a dog cart and a governess cart were used for transport.

The approach to the original Adcott farmhouse was from the north-west but this was changed, and became the tradesmen's entrance. The main drive was constructed from the west using an old farm road and removing part of a plantation. A former pond located close to the house became an ornamental lake.

The original Adcott farm house was incorporated into the new house, so a new Home Farm was built nearby. This would supply milk, cream, butter and cheese to the house. Stables and cow houses were built on the farm. Houses for the staff were built nearby: a laundry, and two lodges at each end of the gated drives. The lodges and cottages were distinctive in style using a dark brick and decorative barge boards. Local farm houses too were extended and improved. The Darbys had made a model estate with an impressive house, lodge houses, parkland and gardens.

With the construction of various cottages for staff, the estate was now complete and ready for occupation. The last responsibility before Rebecca Darby could move was the recruitment of staff to run the house and gardens. Each town had a recruitment agency for all household and estate workers, but few local people were ever selected. According to the census, Rebecca Darby employed a housekeeper, a butler, lady's maid, three housemaids, a cook, kitchen maid, footman and groom. Amazingly not one of the household staff was recruited locally! The staff at Adcote therefore formed a significant influx of population and new blood into the village. The reasoning behind this was that an employer did not want gossip and tittle-tattle in the local community or petty pilfering. However, some young gardeners were selected from local families.

Church

The Chapel of Ease at Little Ness was sited within the bailey of the motte and bailey castle, constructed by the Normans as part of a chain of fortifications along the Welsh border. Until 1840 all burials from this part of the parish took place at the Mother Church in Baschurch. The footpaths, or coffin paths, can still be traced from various parts of the parish to the church.

St. Martin's Church, Little Ness

It was decided in 1840 to improve both the church fabric and the surrounding land. The roof was replaced and the wooden cupola and bell at the western end was replaced with a sandstone bell turret. The old bell was sold to Mr Meers of a London bell foundry for £7 8s. He probably recast a new bell. Over the south-facing Norman doorway a substantial wooden porch was added. The land around the Church was the Vicar's Glebe which was used to keep sheep. This was tidied and, with the visit of the Bishop of

Lichfield, consecrated for burials. Gravel paths were laid to assist the coffin bearers. These improvements cost £250, a cost borne by the parishioners with £100 given by the absentee landowner, Lord Clive.

Lych Gate

With Adcote complete, Rebecca Darby turned her sights on the church. A wall was built around the churchyard with two wicket gates. Further improvements followed. In 1889 *The Border Churchman* contained the following quotation written by the Vicar of Baschurch:

> With very great pleasure a lych gate is to be put at
> the entrance to Little Ness Churchyard and this we
> are indebted to Mr Christy, a brother of Mrs Darby
> of Adcote. The churchyard by reason of its
> situation and by the way it is kept, such as we

rarely see, and this further addition to it will make
it yet more complete. Perhaps we may some day
have a great improvement to our churchyard.

Although the Vicar is acknowledging the generosity of the Christy and Darby families, one can detect an undercurrent of envy for no rich patron living in other parts of the parish was willing to beautify the churchyard of the Mother Church!

A School for Little Ness

Following restoration of the Church, Rebecca Darby decided to build a school. The site of the old village pound was chosen as it was central to the surrounding hamlets. Although the earliest records date from October 1892, the school was probably built in 1875. It was a single storey brick building with just one classroom and a lean-to cloakroom. The lavatories were earth closets situated across the playground. The playground's surface was rough gravel. In the corner was a flagpole.

School (now used as the Village Hall)

Miss Mary Elizabeth Rose was the teacher-in-charge with Nora Badger in charge of the infants. On Tuesday and Thursday mornings the Baschurch Curate taught Religious Instruction. An Inspector visited annually to test the children's knowledge. Once the inspection had finished the rest of the day was granted as a holiday. Certificates were awarded to knowledgeable children, which were greatly prized, many being framed and hung on the wall.

It was not all praise from Her Majesty's Inspector, who, as well as checking the teaching, also inspected the buildings. The boys' 'offices' were not up to standard. He reported them as dirty, having no urinals, the lavatories being used for this purpose. There was a quick response to this criticism, two new closets were built, each separated by a ventilated door, and separate urinals were also constructed.

In 1896 a separate classroom for the Infants was built, with an internal wood and glass partition. When necessary this partition was folded back making a useful larger room. Another HMI considered that the school needed a thermometer, followed later by the suggestion that pictures were needed to brighten up a dark interior. A quick response from the founder Mrs Darby followed:

> We disagree with the Inspector's report. We should have heard more of the work of the school and less about the furnishings. No doubt a picture gallery is instructive, but we should have thought the proper place for the children's eyes were the blackboard, books or the teacher's face. We beg to differ about the gloomy interior.

In due course a large window was inserted in the east wall, thus improving the light for the children working at their desks.

At the end of each May, Empire Day was celebrated. The Darby family always attended the school bringing important guests. The school children were well drilled for the event. They sang patriotic songs, including 'Happy English Children.' At 11.30am everyone gathered around the flagpole and the Union Jack was hoisted. Mr Darby, or a special guest, gave an address. One was entitled 'The Growth and Size of the British Empire.' This was followed by another patriotic song and then the National Anthem. The children formed a line and walked past the flag saluting. Mrs Darby then gave each child a bun and an orange. Before they were free to enjoy these treats, all gave three rousing cheers for The King and the Royal Family and then one for Mrs Darby.

The discipline of the school was not entirely in the Headmistress' hands. If a child's behaviour was really bad this was reported to Mrs Darby. In two cases the behaviour was considered so bad the boys were asked to leave Little Ness and join Baschurch School. There were also times when Alfred Darby caned naughty boys.

Health and welfare

The health of the children was important to Mrs Darby and she was told who was ill. She sent fruit and food, often visiting the patient herself. The author's aunt, as a child, had been unwell and was sent, with another sick child, for a month to Lady Forrester's Convalescent Home in Rhyl - taken there and collected by the chauffeur in the brake!

Both Ruyton and Baschurch had doctors at this time, but many people could not afford to visit them. The ladies of these parishes decided to form a Nursing Association. Mrs Darby was elected as President, Mrs Walford of Ruyton Towers became Vice-President, Mrs Brown of Ruyton Hall the Secretary and Mrs Cunningham, the Doctor's wife, Treasurer. They decided the annual fee for an artisan would be three shillings and for a labourer two shillings. This included the treatment of the whole family. These District Nurses were very skilled in childbirth, accidents in the home and all manner of illnesses. They had large area to cover and so they rode bicycles - their equipment in a large leather bag strapped onto the carrier at the back. The women were called out both day and night. Not having telephones, messages were brought to them by walkers and cyclists. They turned out at all times and in all weathers.

The Darbys, following the fashion, bought cars and they had one for general use. If parishioners had hospital appointments or a visit to the doctor's, a lift could be arranged. The chauffeur had a uniform, a brown double-breasted jacket with brass buttons and brown jodhpurs.

Alfred's marriage

Before Rebecca Darby moved to Adcote both her daughters were married. Alice Mary married Francis Alexander Woolryche-Whitmore. She too was following her father's first cousin, Adelaide, by marrying into the Shropshire gentry, part of the Woolryche-Whitmore family. The Darbys were now accepted gentry. Alfreda Lucy, born after the death of her father, married into the North Shropshire gentry, Hillyer David Chapman, a widower, of Kilhendre, Ellesmere.

With his mother moving into Adcote, Alfred, as heir to the Adcote estate, was an eligible bachelor. The Lloyd family, who lived at Aston Hall, near Oswestry, were friends of the Darby family. Mrs Lloyd was well connected as she was the daughter of the 11th Earl of Kenoull. Her niece, Frederica Louisa Juliana Arthur, daughter of Sir Frederick Arthur and Lady Elizabeth Hay, often stayed with her at Aston Hall. It is said that Alfred met Frederica at a ball given by Mrs Lloyd at Aston Hall. With this impeccable background she was considered an acceptable partner for Alfred. The pair were married in London in 1881.

A daughter, Frances Muriel was born in May 1882. There was a long wait for the son and heir, Alfred Alexander Maurice, who was born in 1894. There was great rejoicing at his birth.

1894 was also the year when Muriel Darby was confirmed into the Church of England. The Bishop of Lichfield agreed to hold a confirmation service in Little Ness Church. A number of village girls of a similar age were also invited to be confirmed too. The author's mother, was one of the girls invited. Mrs Darby overcame any difficulty regarding the village girls' dresses as she provided them. They were dressed in cream, whereas Muriel Darby was dressed in white. When the Bishop 'laid on hands' the village girls knelt at the altar rail but Muriel Darby knelt in front of them at a prix deux! Miss Darby would be recognised at once by the Bishop and God!

Whilst living at Little Ness House, Alfred and Frederica played a minor role in running the church and school. Alfred was Chairman at Coalbrookdale, and as time went on, Frederica, took over Rebecca's village responsibilities.

Rebecca's death

In March 1909 Rebecca Darby died, aged 88 years. The *Shrewsbury Chronicle* report paid tribute to her achievements:

> She was a devoted member of the Church of England. In 1878 she bore the cost of the redecoration of Little Ness Church. Quietly and unobtrusively Mrs Darby did many good works in Little Ness. She was a real benefactress and county philanthropist, agencies received from her generous support and recognition.

Alfred at Adcote

Life in Little Ness parish did not change much after the death of Rebecca Darby. Following her death, Alfred and Frederica moved from Little Ness House to Adcote. Frederica had a larger staff to manage and more local duties to perform. Alfred now had full control over the Adcote Estate and continued as Chairman of the Coalbrookdale Works. Muriel Darby lived at Sunniside in Coalbrookdale, and led a full life in that community.

In 1911, two years after moving into Adcote, Alfred applied to the Church Commissioners for Little Ness to become an independent parish. By an Order of the Church Council it was agreed that Little Ness should become a parish independent of Baschurch. A modern Vicarage was built on land near the school. There was also a convenient footpath connecting the house through Church Farm, to the Church. The Vicarage was completed in 1926. Arthur Evelyn Furnival MA, curate of Baschurch between 1903 and 1911 became the first Vicar of an independent Little Ness.

The First World War

The idyllic life at Adcote and Coalbrookdale came to an abrupt end when war was declared with Germany in 1914. The British Army consisted of volunteers, so men from all walks of life and professions joined one of the services. Women were now very important to the workforce, guided into work that had previously been the domain of men. The world was changing.

Maurice Darby was at Merton College, Oxford, and he with many of his contemporaries volunteered to join the army. He joined the prestigious Grenadier Guards. The Coalbrookdale Archives contain letters he wrote to his parents and relatives whilst serving at the Front in France. They were positive and cheerful for the war was not expected to last long. However, fate intervened as it had many times before, and Maurice was killed at Neieve Chapelle in France just before his 21st birthday. This was a

The Darby graves at Little Ness

devastating blow to his parents. Usually casualties of war were buried in a war graves cemetery. However, contrary to convention, Maurice's uncle, Sir George Arthur, was allowed onto the battlefield to search for the body. Once found, he returned with it to Little Ness. One can speculate that perhaps special dispensation was granted because Maurice Darby was Queen Mary's godson.

The following account appeared in a local newspaper:

> The small church at Little Ness was the scene of a full military funeral. Eight sergeants and twenty-two drummers from his regiment of the Grenadier Guards headed the funeral procession to the grave. The eight sergeants acted as Pall Bearers, while the fifes and drums played Chopin's Funeral March.

The grave was lined with moss and daffodils. Alfred and Frederica, his parents, laid wreaths on the coffin. Maurice was laid to rest near the south door of the church with his Christy relatives. With his death went all his parents' plans for the future as Squire of the Adcote Estate. He was the last direct male heir to this branch of the Darby family.

The north window in the church was used to commemorate his death. It has a stained glass window depicting the fighting saints, St George, St Maurice and St Michael. The inscription beneath reads:

> In the Glorious Hope and Resurrection and Loving Memory of Maurice Darby, who died in battle for his country, March 11th 1915, this window is dedicated by his parents, Alfred and Frederica Darby.

From the field of battle, the company drum was brought back with his body. This was placed on the south window ledge. It was a poignant reminder of war and death but also a very distinctive reminder of battles past.

In her intense grief, Frederica Darby decided to help the soldiers on the Front practically. In October 1916 she left Britain for France joining a working party of the YMCA. She joined a section run under the auspices of the American Red Cross and worked with them until March 1917. She had chosen to work during the winter months when life would not have been easy for the soldiers or volunteer helpers.

Frederica returned to Adcote to a quieter country life. Her daughter, Muriel, was now 37 years old and settled at Sunniside, Coalbrookdale. To everyone's surprise her engagement was announced to Captain Mordant Lackenby-Cope of Bramshall, Hampshire. He belonged to a country gentry family who were of the Roman Catholic faith.

The wedding was to take place on 17 July 1917. A London house was rented, 26 Wilton Crescent. On the eve of the wedding Mr and Mrs Darby gave a reception where the wedding gifts were displayed. As was common in those days a wedding list was published. The gifts included a pair of diamond and pearl drop earrings from the bridegroom to the bride, a gold watch in a gunmetal case from the bride to the bridegroom, a diamond tiara, an amethyst and diamond necklace and ear-rings, a platinum wrist watch surrounded by diamonds from Frederica Darby and a diamond and platinum slide on old velvet, a canteen of silver, a set of George II table candlesticks, a silver tea set and salver from Alfred Darby. The Adcote staff gave the couple a silver cigar box inscribed as follows: 'To Miss Darby, We the undersigned indoor and outdoor staff at Adcote, beg your acceptance of the accompanying cigar box on the occasion of your marriage. July 17 1917.'

Following their wedding, the married couple left for their honeymoon at Adcote. It was a brief honeymoon, as Captain Cope was to leave with his regiment for Egypt on 27 July. Muriel Darby returned to Coalbrookdale, to live at Sunniside. Sadly the marriage did not last and Muriel decided to be known in future as Mrs Cope-Darby.

When war ended and the soldiers returned, a party was held at Adcote to welcome them home. Each received a silver topped walking stick. Photographs of the men, including local hero Tom Davies who received the Military Medal, were distributed to all local residents. Many of the returning soldiers did not remain in the area for they found work further afield.

Sadly, seven local men lost their lives during the conflict and it was subsequently decided to erect a War Memorial in the centre of the village. The cross was made from local sandstone and was paid for by public subscription. The men who died had their names engraved on it along with others who had left the village to serve in HM forces.

'Welcome Home' party held at Adcote

'Welcome Home' party

A Royal Visitor

Alfred and Frederica Darby had a great lift to their spirits on 15 August 1921 when Queen Mary and her daughter, the Princess Royal, visited them at Adcote. This caused great excitement in the area. A number of photographs were taken and one of Queen Mary standing by a pillar looking out at the garden at Adcote was distributed widely throughout the parish. Not many Shropshire houses had this distinction.

Queen Mary at Adcote, 1921

Tragedy and a sale

Mrs Frederica Darby was a popular local figure and was invited to open many bazaars, sales of work and other money-raising good causes in the area. On 20 July 1925 she had been invited to open a fete in Ellesmere. If Alfred was at home when his wife was out, he would open the door to welcome her home. On this occasion, she was surprised when the Butler received her. He was the carrier of bad news, for while she was in Ellesmere, Alfred had died. This was a terrible shock as he had not been ill. He was 75, much older than some of his direct male ancestors. He was taken for burial to Coalbrookdale to the church which his father (Alfred), uncle (Abraham IV), and their sister, Mary, had built in Ironbridge.

Muriel Cope-Darby, Alfred's daughter, was his immediate and only descendent. She was still living at Sunniside in Coalbrookdale. She did not want the Adcote estate, so she decided to put it up for sale. The only exclusion was Little Ness House so that her mother Frederica could return to the house where she spent the early years of her marriage. The estate was to be sold on 6 October 1926. Existing tenants were given the option to buy their farms and houses. Many tenants took advantage of this offer and found they were paying less in mortgage than they had been paying in rent.

Adcote did not attract an English buyer. Too many families had lost their sons and heirs during the war and many large houses and their accompanying estates were put up for sale in the post war period. Money was short as the country was suffering from economic depression. Eventually an American buyer decided to buy the property and ship it 'stone by stone' to America. Local people were horrified. Workmen were sent to mark the stones in preparation for rebuilding. As in fairytale endings to stories, at the very last moment an English buyer was found. Not a family but a consortium of people prepared to open a girl's school.

Adcote enters a new era

Mr and Mrs Gough from Shifnal needed larger premises to expand their flourishing school. The Goughs were urged to visit the property quickly before the American deal was finalised. They came to Adcote and Mrs

Gough's immediate reaction on seeing it was, 'it's just what we need.' 10% of the asking price was requested, £910 being the deposit. A Limited Company was formed with Mrs Gough as Chairman and Miss Gough as Secretary. The largest owners of ordinary shares were Mrs Gough, Miss Gough, Mrs Cope-Darby and Mr Kidson of Weston Manor in Wolverhampton. Four other people were allotted preference shares. Mrs Cope-Darby with her business acumen and generosity helped the Gough family to buy Adcote. This was the perfect solution for the future of Adcote.

Mrs Frederica Darby, in the meantime was on holiday in Brittany. On hearing the news of the sale, she wrote at once to Mrs Gough:

> It was a real pain to think of Adcote being pulled
> down, and now, thank God, that is not to be, and
> it is quite true that of all things in the world I
> wanted to come to Adcote was a school, so I got
> my wish in every way.

Few local people realised that Mrs Cope-Darby was so involved in the future of Adcote. The school opened in September 1927 with 60 pupils and more followed in January 1928. Not many alterations were needed. The large servants' room on the top floor was made into the Big Bathroom. This had three baths and a line of washbasins with screens in between. A new water pump was installed as far more water would be needed for this new, much enlarged community.

It was important that the school should be as near self-sufficient in fruit, vegetables, plants and flowers as possible. Haughton, the old school, was still unsold, so was able to provide Adcote from its kitchen gardens. Mr Clampit, the Head Gardener at Haughton transferred to Adcote. He lived in the South Lodge at the end of the drive. Both he and Mrs Clampit remained there for the rest of their lives. He became a well-known judge at local flower and vegetable shows.

The Darby's Garden Room was renovated and turned into a gymnasium. This was completed and equipped by the end of the summer term 1928. A service was taken by the Vicars of Little Ness and Great Ness outside the building and Mrs Frederica and Mrs Cope-Darby were given a silver key to unlock the door. A gymnastic display followed. The school flourished and by the summer of 1929 there were 72 boarders.

Girl Guides always played an important part in school life and in the surrounding area. A Guide Company was formed in Baschurch in the mid-1920s by Miss Blantyrn of Church House. When the family left the district, Adcote School stepped in to run the Company. This proved a very successful move and the Company flourished. Miss Hazell was Captain, a very likable person who always gave sound advice. Other staff and senior girls helped to run the meetings and took girls camping. Margaret Timmis from the Merehouse in Baschurch, a pupil and local farmer's daughter, became Lieutenant. Her friends, Kathleen Wathes and Miss Ferrand joined the camps. Miss Gough often visited and knew everyone well. Village girls had much to thank Miss Gough and her Guiders. The Baschurch Guides were invited to follow the Adcote guides on camping trips. The author can recall a trip to Anglesey where each girl was instructed to take a clean sack and pillow case. When we arrived these were filled with straw and became our mattress and pillow! A very enjoyable holiday – thanks to Miss Gough.

On a Sunday, the Church of England girls would walk to Little Ness church in crocodile fashion, dressed in green coats with green velour hats. Special services were held for the school because the Adcote girls filled the small church completely. Mr Gough however was a keen Methodist, so he attended Baschurch Methodist Chapel taking with him any girls who wished to worship there.

Mr Gough did not play an active part in running the school as an educational establishment, but was in charge of all the outdoor staff. On 19 June 1930 he went to visit his sister who was ill in Shifnal. The next day, news arrived that she had passed away. Very sadly, later that same day, Mr Gough suffered a massive stroke and he too died - a great shock to his wife and daughter.

Frederica Darby remembered

Frederica's daughter, Muriel Cope-Darby, died at Coalbrookdale at the age of 53. She was the last in the line of that particular branch of the Darby family. She was brought to Little Ness to be buried with her brother. After Muriel died, Frederica was left with few close relatives. Her brother, Sir George Arthur was still alive but he was now elderly. Her great-niece, Lady Rachel Labouchere, and her niece, Beryl Chapman, were her closest Darby relations. Mrs Darby engaged a companion, Dorothy Doughty, from Coalbrookdale, who was probably was a friend of Muriel Cope-Darby. She took charge of Mrs Darby's welfare and the running of Little Ness House.

Following Alfred's death, Mrs Darby made a number of alterations to the church in her husband's memory. Three carved chairs, one dating to 1648, were donated. The stout oak beam across the centre of the church was transferred into a Rood beam. In the centre was a crucifix of Christ, supported by Our Lady and John on one side and two angels on the other. The inscription read: 'In glorious hope of the Resurrection and in loving memory of Alfred E.W. Darby this Rood is given by his wife in the year of our Lord, 1927. Requisat in Pace.'

In 1931 she gave a Processional Cross made in oak, with a sacred monogram and the arms of St Martin. The following year, the old bier, which had to be carried on the shoulders of the bearers, was replaced with a more modern wheeled bier, making the coffin bearers task a little easier as they made their way up the steep churchyard path.

Mrs Darby was genuinely interested in the wellbeing of the village community. Peter Davies recalls that on his and his twin sister's eighth birthday in 1936, Mrs Darby appeared at the school and asked to withdraw Peter and Daphne. Mystified, he and his sister walked along the road with her to their farmhouse. On seeing his father hanging over the gate, she shouted, 'It's a birthday Tom.' There was little reaction from his father. On reaching the gate leading to the front door, Mrs Darby opened it. (Peter recalls the only other person to use the front door was the Vicar.) His mother, equally surprised, opened the door to the trio. She took them into the front room, where they were seated. The front room was never visited by the children and tea was brought in the best china cups. Mrs Darby then gave each a present. Peter remembers his book was, *Pip, Squeak and Wilfred.* He has no idea to this day why they were chosen to have birthday presents from Mrs Darby. In later years, Peter became a very competent pianist and was invited, when Mrs Darby had visitors to entertain, to play on the Bechstein piano. When Mrs Darby died his mother bought the Bechstein for him at the sale.

Another example of Mrs Darby's interest in local people occurred when the author reached the age of five and was about to start school. Mrs Darby visited my mother to find out why I was going to attend Baschurch School rather than the school in Little Ness. The reason was explained; that at such a young age, it was too far and lonely to walk to Little Ness, but, if I attended Baschurch School, there were other children to walk with. Of course my mother and her family plus other children had walked daily to Little Ness School. However, by this time, no other children from Milford went to Little Ness.

Frederica Darby, 1939

Life changed dramatically in 1939 with the outbreak of the Second World War. A number of Mrs Darby's staff had to leave, either to join the Forces or take up war work. Many women in the area chose to become Land Girls.

The house had fewer servants and gardeners and as a result the gardens and hot houses suffered. Food was not easily obtained and most goods were rationed so the gardens were used to grow vegetables. Fuel was rationed for the cars, so shopping and visits were restricted. There was an influx of mothers and children from Birkenhead into the parish but none were directed to Little Ness House.

The evacuees must have found life in Little Ness and the surrounding hamlets very strange. No artificial lights, just oil lamps and candles; no water lavatories in the back yard but a trip down the garden to a smelly earth closet. No running water or street lights. The children were registered at the school and attendance was recorded on a separate register.

On one occasion during wartime, the local postman, after delivering letters to the back door of Little Ness House, reported to everyone he met that he had seen Mrs Darby sitting on a bench in the sunshine plucking a pheasant! She ran meetings in her house to make comforts for the Forces. Gloves, scarves, balaclavas and mittens were made and whist drives were held to raise money for wool.

The school was not over looked for Mrs Darby always paid a Christmas visit. No longer were the Christmas gifts warm jumpers and lengths of material, as clothing was rationed. Instead money was given with each child receiving a florin (two shillings) or half-a crown (two shillings six pence) if they were in the church choir. Mr and Mrs Hignett also contributed, giving each child one shilling. Mr and Mrs Hignett had left Liverpool because of the heavy bombing raids and lived at the North Lodge, on the Adcote Estate. It was said he was a tobacco millionaire. Each week he and his wife had a taxi to Shrewsbury, to the George Hotel, where they had a weekly bath as there was no running water or electricity in the village.

Liverpool was 60 miles away, but German bombers flew over the village to bomb the docks. The intense fires could be seen from vantage points in the village. A searchlight post was placed along the Nibs Heath road, just south of Quality Square and was manned by two soldiers. Further along the road an airfield was built at Forton Heath. The men were housed at Grafton and Fitz in huts. Milford Bridge, the crossing point of the River Perry, had a defensive structure built on the Little Ness side of the river. This was manned by the local Home Guard but they never saw any action!

Finally the war came to an end, but unfortunately there were no VE day celebrations as there was an outbreak of whooping cough in the area affecting many families. Later, in October, the parishes of Little Ness and Great Ness combined having a 'Welcome Home Party' in Great Ness Village Hall.

Local parishioners recall that Mrs Darby would often be seen at church, dressed in black and with a bunch of parma violets attached to her coat. She would attend the Matins service on Sunday mornings sitting with the remnants of the choir until shortly before the sermon, when she would walk to the front seat near the pulpit and dramatically produce a large ear trumpet to listen to the sermon!

Mrs Darby visited Little Ness School on 18 March 1946. The Log Book records her final visit. On 26 March, she died in her sleep. The school log book records: 'She was a personal friend to every child.' Frederica Darby, or 'Rica' as she signed herself, was buried with her husband in a grave near the Church door. Many parishioners attended her funeral. She had lived in Little Ness for 65 years outliving her son, daughter and husband. She did not die rich, either in money or property. She left legacies to her faithful employees who had been with her many years; her companion, Miss Doughty; her chauffeur, George McChesney; the Head Gardener, Alf Yeomans; the cook and housemaid. Her custom made Austin 16 motor car she left to her chauffeur - a very thoughtful gesture. He was able to use it as a taxi for the rest of his working life!

With the death of Frederica Darby, this appeared to be the end of the Darby connection with Little Ness. However, a surprise find came to light soon after Little Ness House was sold.

A surprise find!

Local lady, Ruth Cook, was discussing the Darby family with the author when she revealed a strange episode in her life. After Frederica's death and the estate had been sold, her uncle took her to Little Ness House to view the property he had bought. In the harness room, they discovered a metal uniform case. The case contained the Grenadier Guards uniform belonging to the late Maurice Darby. Ruth, carefully made a written record of everything she saw:

> We went into the room, my father and two of my uncles, my cousin and my grandfather and started to look around. The first thing brought to light by my cousin, Elizabeth, in a tin box, were things called epaulettes, there was a rose on each one of them and sort of tassels hanging down made of silver wire.

> Then we unearthed many things, a red coat of beautiful cloth, very closely woven and lovely buttons and a lot of gold braid, and trousers to match with no turn-ups and a red stripe down the leg. Also a cloak of rather coarser material lined with red and fastened with two Tudor roses, there were many Tudor roses adorning the other clothes. Elizabeth found and put on a sumptuous

black coat, similar to the red except that on the shoulders there was a sort of twisted braid with two different stars to denote the rank. There were trousers to match this coat with gold stripes down the leg.

We decided from the clothes that the son of Alfred (Maurice Darby) was extremely tall and slim, for the trousers were very long and the coats not at all broad. He had small feet, size seven, for there were two pairs of riding boots, one patent leather, the other ordinary leather.

In a piece of tissue paper there were two pairs of exquisite white gloves. There was a white leather belt and a red leather one to go with the red coat covered with gold braid, and two straps hanging down form the belt for the sword. There were three belts, all together, another one was red and gold not as good. There were three purses of silver and two of red with lovely monograms on them. They were oblong and about an inch thick and five inches long. There was a broad blue ribbon with gold tassels which went over one shoulder and under the other one, we were not sure what this was for.

The most magnificent and striking of all these things were the hats. There were two small little hats that go on the side of the head with a piece of elastic under the chin. There was a high sheriffs hat, a long affair with a plume of white feathers

> and part of the badge. There was a silver one, very beautiful. On the silver a pattern in the middle a star and 'Shropshire Yeomanry.' This had a red and white plume in a separate tin. There was a chain to go under the chin.

Sadly, Ruth does not know what happened to this amazing discovery but at least we have her excellent description of this wonderful find.

The valuable paintings!

The final Darby connection to Little Ness relates to paintings which used to hang on the east wall in the church. For many years no particular interest was shown in these works of art. The Reverend Parrot, in his book on the history of Little Ness, published in 1935, simply describes them as 'old Flemish paintings.'

However, during the mid-1950s, Nicholas Pevsner, was travelling throughout England, carrying out research in order to compile a series of books on *The Buildings of England.* At this time he was a Professor of Fine Arts at the Slade in London. Upon visiting the church in Little Ness, he was surprised to find a number of paintings. Following his visit, Pevsner wrote to the Vicar suggesting the paintings should be examined by experts in London as they could be of great value. The Vicar felt they should be examined in situ as they were the PCC's responsibility, and to transport them to London would involve a hefty insurance which the PCC could not afford. In the event, no further action was taken and the paintings were left where they were. Pevsner's volume on Shropshire, published in 1958, describes the paintings as 'German, early sixteenth century triptych in early nineteenth century English frames.'

Nothing further occurred until the Reverend Bradbury was appointed Vicar of Little Ness in 1983. Interested in art himself, Rev. Bradbury realised the paintings were possibly important works of art. At this point in time the village needed affordable housing and the church was in need of repair. With very little money and no rich patron, the Church needed to find a source of money. So with ecclesiastical approval, Rev. Bradbury asked Sotheby's to send an expert to view the paintings. Sotheby's felt that the paintings were painted by the same artist, had originally formed a triptych and would probably sell for a large sum. The main panel showed 'The Entombment of Christ' and the two wings showed St Christopher and St George. Experts suggested the paintings should be sold as two lots in order to maximise their value. At the sale in 1993, the central panel fetched £232,500 and the wings £40,000. The paintings were purchased by foreign buyers.

The proceeds from the sale were used to build two affordable houses for couples having connections with Little Ness. The rest of the money was used for Church repairs and the upkeep of the Churchyard. However, the story does not end there, for the paintings came up for sale again in the late 1990s. The main panel was purchased by the National Galleries of Scotland and is now housed in Edinburgh, and the wings were purchased by the Peter Moore Foundation and can be seen in Compton Verney Gallery in Warwickshire. Research into the paintings has continued into the twenty-first century as art experts and historians have tried to work out the possible artist.

Back in 1993, Sotheby's believed the paintings had originally been purchased by a member of the Darby family in the early part of the nineteenth century and, as the paintings were recorded in a church inventory of 1909, had probably been given to the Church during the last quarter of the nineteenth century during improvements to the building by Rebecca Darby. However, *The Border Churchman* for January 1906 states: 'Mr Alfred Darby gave four paintings ... to the Church.' Surprisingly, the paintings were not hung in the church for a number of years for a photograph of the interior dating to 1911 does not show them hanging at the eastern end.

A former churchwarden at Little Ness, Mrs Joan Gregory, was told by Alf Yeomans, Mrs Darby's former gardener, that he had originally brought the paintings from Sunniside in Coalbrookdale and that they were only hung in the church in 1928, after Mr Alfred Darby's decease.

It would seem likely that the original purchaser was Francis Darby, but sadly some of his later account books do not survive and there is no written evidence of his purchase. However, his art collection remained at Sunniside after his death when the house passed to his wife Hannah, his daughter Adelaide and finally to his eldest daughter Matilda. Following her death in 1902, the house was inherited by Alfred Darby II.

It is with the discovery and sale of the paintings that our story of the Darbys concludes: the journey of a family from nationally renowned Iron Masters in Coalbrookdale to country landowners in Little Ness.

Publications:

C. Cluley, 'Discovery of a Lost Masterpiece', paper written for the Nuremburg Art Conference (2012).

Sandys Birket Foster, *The Pedigrees of Dickinson of Gildersome and Coalbrookdale; Darby of Coalbrookdale, Salop; Darby of Stoke Court Bucks* (Privately printed, 1890).

T. Hill, 'Bather Family of Adcote'

R. Lowe, *The History of Adcote School* (Shrewsbury, 1987).

Rev. P.A. Parrott, *Little Ness: The Story of a Shropshire Parish* (Shrewsbury, 1935).

A. Raistrick, *Dynasty of Ironfounders: The Darbys and Coalbrookdale* (Newton Abbot, 1989).

Rev. Rice 'Little Ness' (pamphlet)

T. Rowley, *The Shropshire Landscape* (London, 1972).

A. Saint, *Norman Shaw* (Rhode Island, 1977; new edition 2010).

M.A. Scard, *The Building Stones of Shropshire* (Shrewsbury, 1990).

B. Trinder, *The Darbys of Coalbrookdale* (Chichester, 1991).

Victoria County History of Shropshire, volumes II and XI.

Diaries:

E. Thomas (ed), *The Private Journal of Adelaide Darby of Coalbrookdale, 1833-1861,* transcribed by R. Labouchere (York, 2004).

R. Labouchere, *Abiah Darby, 1716-1793, of Coalbrookdale* (York, 1988).

R. Labouchere, *Deborah Darby of Coalbrookdale, 1754-1810,* (York, 1993).

The Diary of Hannah Rose (unpublished).

Primary Sources (available at Shropshire Archives):

Little Ness Tithe Maps, Little Ness Church Records, Casey's Shropshire Directory 1851 & 1861, Ellesmere Rural District Church Magazines: *The Border Churchman*

Local Newspapers: *Shrewsbury Chronicle, Wellington Journal*

Personal reminiscences:

Lady Labouchere, Mrs Eva Garmston, Mrs Eileen George, Mrs Joan Gregory, Mr George McChesney, Mr Peter Davies and the author herself.